1001 ways to make money

1001 ways to make money

By L J Pearce

Hillside Publishing

Published by Hillside Publishing
66 Hillside Road
Linton
Swadlincote
Derbyshire
DE12 6QW
www.1001waystomakemoney.co.uk

The author has done her best to present accurate and up-to-date information in this book, but she cannot guarantee that this information is correct or will suit your particular situation. This book is sold with the understanding that the publisher and the author are not engaged in rendering legal, accounting or any other professional services. If expert assistance is needed or required the services of a professional should be sought.

ISBN-13: 978-0-9561078-0-0

Note: The material contained in this book is set out in good faith for general guidance and no liability can be accepted for loss or expense incurred as a result of relying on particular circumstances on statements made in this book. The laws and regulations are complex and liable to change, and readers should check the current position with the relevant authorities before making personal arrangements.

1001 Ways to make money
Contents page

Acknowledgments

I would like to say a big thank you to everyone that helped me research this book, this includes my ever suffering family and the love of my life Brendan. Thank you for your support and advice, and constant nagging this book is dedicated to you.

Introduction

Welcome to 1001 ways to make money. This book is aimed at helping you make some extra money. It includes using skills and knowledge that you already have, alongside skills and qualifications you could gain in the future.

To successfully make money you have to plan what you want to do and why, you have to enjoy something to really succeed in it. Hopefully this book will get you started making more money.

This book covers ways to make and save money, as well as including handy chapters on how to create multiple income streams, and how to make your money work for you.

Believe in yourself and your capabilities and please enjoy reading and using this book.

www.1001waystomakemoney.co.uk

Plus find FREE money making and money saving articles at:
www.associatedcontent.com/user/62651/l_j_pearce.html

How to use this book

What this book is not - a get rich scheme, a promise to make you millions over night without you having to even lift a finger.

What this book is - 1001 ideas to help you make some extra money, a book that helps you save and earn money (hopefully at the same time).

How to use this book - try to use this book as a reference. It is not a money maker on its own; you have to start the ball rolling. You have to accept that you cannot put every idea into action at the same time, this will lead to failure. Use the ideas in this book, but use them as guidelines, evaluate each idea and amend it to suit you and your needs.

Please make notes while reading this book, as I am sure your brain will be working when reading, and so you will probably come up with spin-off ideas which will in turn be their own money making ideas.

Happy Reading!

Chapter 1 - Ways to make money 1-100

1. Hold healthy eating classes.
For example you could do this at your local community centre. A lot of people don't know where to start when it comes to living a more healthy life, so why not show them the way. Your local council may be able to provide you with leaflets based around healthy eating etc that you can pass on to your clients. You could hold weekly healthy eating and living sessions, perhaps 2 -3 times a week and at £1.00 + a head, (dependant on the demand, and the area you are in).
PROS: There is a market for healthy eating and living, as people seem to have less time to focus on their diets and habits.
CONS: This money making idea, may be time consuming and you may have to talk to health practitioners etc, to make sure you are giving people the correct advice.

2. Learn how to mix cocktails and then teach others.
Buy a second hand cocktail mixing book and get to work. Once you have mastered the art of mixing cocktails, you can sell your knowledge as well as selling your fresh homemade cocktails.
PROS: Low cost money making idea to set up.
CONS: You might be subject to local health regulations and you may be tempted to drink the cocktails yourself!

3. Teach people how to host dinner parties.
Advertise your services to individuals or businesses, and teach them what to do and what not to do when holding a dinner party, in order to make it a success. You could target both individuals and small businesses.
PROS: It has low start-up costs. Experience is required, if you are inexperienced in this area then host a party or two, see how you get on and take it from there.
CONS: You may get invited to a lot of dinner parties.

4. Sell clothing for larger women and men.
Sell by mail order, or perhaps online, this can be a weekend, part time or a fulltime money making idea. The world is your marketplace, and you can run this from your home.
PROS: They are products that are always in demand.
CONS: May have start-up costs of £100+ due to buying stock and advertising the business/service.

5. How about being an exhibitions designer.

6. Create/start a baby naming service.
This could include you finding out the history of a babies name for a fee. You could advertise at hospitals, doctors surgeries, mother and parent groups, nurseries etc. You could also sell items that are personalised with babies' names.
PROS: Babies are always being born.
CONS: You have to enjoy socialising and being surrounded by everything to do with babies.

7. Learn how to make and sell children's furniture.
For example creating safari inspired furniture, and then selling direct to customers or on to wholesalers and shops.
PROS: There are always children and parents who need furniture, for example you could have repeat customers, as the children get older and want new furniture.
CONS: You will have to get advice from your local council as to what regulations you must follow to make and sell children's furniture.

8. Teach people how to write their own book.
Fancy yourself as a bit of a writer? Then why not hold book writing classes. Perhaps you could offer classes over the internet, in your home or as a one to one tutorial. Or you could even hold group classes at you local community centre.
PROS: Low start-up costs.
CONS: Writing experience required alongside good knowledge of the English language, punctuation, grammar and so on.

9. Sell clothes, accessories for premature/small babies.
Specialise in selling these perhaps by mail order in your local area, or you could advertise using word of mouth.

10. Help people set up a business.
You could charge people a daily or hourly rate. As an alternative, If you didn't want to help people set up a business you could always just sell them information on how to set up a business, for example, provide them with business contacts for their local area, provide mailing lists, useful contacts etc.
TOP TIP: Get in touch with your local press/media to generate coverage.
TOP TIP: Even if you have never run a business before you could help people fill out forms, help advertise their business, or just be a PA as and when required.

11. Open a vegetarian restaurant/vegetarian takeaway.
Just like opening a normal takeaway but with a twist - a vegetarian one, people are more health conscious and this could be a niche within your area. If you wanted to you could also offer this service alongside healthy eating classes.

12. Sell animal friendly products.
You could set up a mail order company selling products such as leather free handbags and shoes, or sell them on a market stall/kiosk.
PROS: Saving animals lives, offering alternatives to leather, could possibly be cheaper to source and buy.
CONS: You may have to do a bit of market research to determine what will sell and what might not.

13. Sell dancewear.
You could sell these products through mail-order or perhaps online. Sell dancewear ranging from leotards to tap shoes, or you could perhaps specify and specialise in one or two popular products. Create your own niche if you prefer and for example sell unique one off dance costumes.

14. Sell babies/children's christening items.
You could for example specialise in selling gift sets and clothing for that special occasion. Why not sell products through mail order, an online boutique/shop or perhaps through retailers if you choose to design and make the items yourself.
TOP TIP: Advertise at local playgroups, hospitals (if possible) and in your local press.

15. Sell personalised accessories for people of all ages, from belts to necklaces and bracelets.
Items for personalisation can be bought from local craft shops, markets or from online boutiques. The items to be personalised can either be provided by the client or bought by you from wholesalers.

16. Buy and sell second-hand antique jewellery.
You could try your hand at buying jewellery from auctions and resell, or source your jewellery from car boots.
PROS: There is serious money to be made, all you have to do is keep you eyes peeled. You can learn a lot about antique jewellery through watching TV programmes, or reading books on buying and selling jewellery.
CONS: Knowledge of the value of jewellery, alongside perhaps experience and knowledge of hallmarks.

17. Become a substitute/supply teacher.
To be a supply teacher you need to be professional and prepared to face any type of classroom situation, why not contact you local council and schools and see what they are looking for in supply teachers.
PROS: Good money, not a full time teaching job, flexible.
CONS: You need to be available at a minutes notice.

18. Be a holiday representative.

19. Become a semi professional or professional Sportsperson.

What was or is your favourite sport? why not turn your sporting hobby into a money making opportunity. To be a professional or semi professional sportsperson, dedication and passion is the number one requirement alongside fitness.

PROS: If you get well known in your field/sport you could earn some serious money.

CONS: Most professional sportspeople tend to retire around the age of 35.

20. Create your own magazine, online or paper based.

With this money making opportunity there are two routes you could take. The first route is to start your own magazine from scratch, and the second is to invest your money into an already up and running magazine franchise such as http://www.my-mag-uk.com for example. Whichever option you choose, make sure you do your research to ensure your magazine has a target market, at the same time as making you a profit.

PROS: Low cost to start and run an online magazine.

CONS: Sometimes hard to get noticed if you don't specialise or have a large enough niche to cover your costs.

21. Start a company or a business that makes products out of recycled materials.

If you are a bit crafty you could create and sell unique pieces and sell at market stalls, online etc. Or you could go around collecting materials which you feel will be useful to make items for peoples homes. If you are not so creative/crafty why not just collect materials and then sell them onto artists/crafters etc.

PROS: You can make some individual, unique and useful pieces.

CONS: Might be a little time consuming collecting or finding suitable materials, which can be reused.

22. Start a business that specialises in providing gift lists for weddings, birthdays, parties and christenings.
With this opportunity you could offer a customised service. Work directly with clients to create wedding lists, once created you could distribute the lists to your client's friends and family, charge a fee for creating and delivering the gift lists by hand (personal touch is always nicer).

23. Sell customised work wear.
You can buy the work wear/uniforms from wholesalers as required, and then add the embroidery or logo onto the clothing. You could make and hand out flyers to local businesses, to build up your own service/business.
PROS: Most companies need uniforms, especially small start-up businesses.
CONS: You may get large orders and have to hire temporary/additional staff.

24. Be a Sports physiotherapist.

25. Start a business or a website that provides a holiday home search.
Why not be the first and only place people go to find a holiday home rental, specialise in one or two areas, do not cover the whole country or the world, people will prefer to visit your site if they know exactly what is on offer.
TOP TIP: If this took off why not offer a permanent holiday home search in addition to offering rentals.

26. Hold parent and baby fitness classes.
Hold classes at your local community hall/school etc. You could charge either by the hour or by the session, parents will love this as it keeps them fit while allowing them to spend time with their children/babies and form a bond.
PROS: More parents are looking to spend time with their children. You could hold classes any day of the week.
CONS: You have to enjoy spending time with children.

27. Offer a translation service.

Ok, so this is a bit specialised but you don't actually have to speak a second language. You could get around this by hiring temporary, seasonal, and occasional workers to do the translations, as and when required. Or perhaps you could get home workers on board, they could produce the translations from their own homes. You could simply forward the translation onto the client. This is a good business as if you use home workers you are minimising your overheads.

28. Sell office products from desks to pens and pencils.

You could do this through mail-order or through an online shop. You can act as a bit of a stationery store. You do not have the overheads of having a physical shop/location, which bumps up traditional stationery stores prices.

PROS: Low start-up costs. Lots of people from individuals to companies require stationary.

CONS: Might be initially difficult to enter the market as there may be bigger companies. You can however offer a more friendly service which is always worth paying extra for.

29. Sell sports equipment targeted towards women.

Women are equals and are playing professional sports and so deserve top quality sports equipment and clothing that fits them and their sport. For example women footballers have different shape and size feet to men, and yet there are only a few companies who provide specially designed women's football boots. If the products don't exist why not consider inventing a product or coming up with an idea for a product and approaching already established players/businesses in the market. Fear not though, you don't have to invent a product, you could simply source manufacturers and wholesalers, and then resell the products, at a profit of course.

TOP TIP: Advertise in women's magazines, you can advertise to both individuals and sports clubs/groups.

30. Design logos, for businesses and individuals.

You can charge by the hour or by the size of the project. If you didn't want to design the logos you could act as an intermediary between the client and logo designer, you could charge a commission for arranging the sale/providing the contacts.

TOP TIP: Advertise in business magazines, business centres, and in online discussion forums.

31. Open a funky/alternative hair salon.

This could for example specialise in dreadlocks or rainbow coloured hair, just something a bit different, you don't have to be a qualified stylist, you could open a hair salon and then employ stylists for example.

PROS: You get to start and provide a creative service, which is sure to attract attention.

CONS: Will need trained stylists, or you will need to be a stylist/hairdresser yourself.

32. Sell clothing and accessories for pets and pet lovers.

More and more people are pet conscious, and like their pets to be just as pampered as they are, so why not cater to this need and start an online doggy boutique or a mail order catalogue that sells pets clothing, including doggy coats, and ferret wear, you could offer products sourced from all over the world. If you didn't want to source supplies or wholesalers you could have a go at creating you own pet clothing line.

TOP TIP: You could offer a custom design pet clothing service. You could offer stock and sell your products through local markets, fetes and pet shops.

33. Why not train or learn to be a dietician.

34. Sell clothing and accessories for people who like dressing up.

For example sell through mail order or through an online shop, you could sell products ranging from underwear to shoes.

35. Sell extreme sports clothing and equipment

You could sell these through mail order or an online shop.

PROS: More people are taking part in extreme sports, so there could be a potentially large target market.

CONS: You may need, or have to hire someone with experience in equipment, as people may ask questions, regarding the safety and use of the equipment.

36. Sell equipment and accessories for horses.

You could do this by mail order, online, or at local markets. To differentiate yourself even more from the competition you could even sell custom riding equipment and tack.

TOP TIP: Advertise at riding schools.

37. Open a Supermarket.

This could be a small online supermarket or a physical location, the choice is yours. Perhaps differentiate by selling products from different continents/countries to cater to multiple groups of people could be your niche.

PROS: You could offer a wide variety of products from across the world.

CONS: May have larger start-up costs than most money making ideas.

38. Become a personal shopper.

What better way to earn money than to go shopping.

You could advertise your service in your local newspaper, alongside fees/rates.

TOP TIP: Offer people a personal file of clothing which may suit them and their body shape.

39. Bake.

Can you bake? Do you enjoy it, if so what about selling homemade cakes/cookies/biscuits either direct or perhaps through shops, and local markets. You could offer cakes for parties, local businesses, conferences, events etc, the list is virtually unlimited.

TOP TIP: Check what health and safety regulations are applicable with your local council.

40. Babysitting/Childcare.

This is ideal for earning that extra bit of money on the side. Place adverts in your local paper/local shops, build up a reputation and then you can build up your fees and hours if you want to. You will need to consider whether you want to be a babysitter whereby you visit peoples homes, or whether you want to become a registered childminder.

TOP TIP: Contact your local council and ask them for further information on rules and regulations regarding caring/looking after children.

41. Create a website and make money by getting people to advertise on your site.

I'm not saying create just an advertising website, as if you solely provide advertising you wont have any content (which is of course what attracts and gets you your visitors).
Build up the number of site visitors you get and you can build up your income, remember quality content = your income.

TOP TIP: Release free press releases, and send to magazines, papers etc to get your site noticed.

42. Be a Money broker.

43.Help people fill in VAT/Tax returns.
How about being a form filler. Some people need a bit of help filling in forms, or just understanding sections of long forms, you could be just the person.
Charge a fee based on the number of forms you help them fill in, or charge people based on time spent e.g. charge by the hour.

44. Organise painting holidays.
Find people who run painting courses, you become the middle man/woman, source clients for the people who run the courses and source painting holiday/trips for clients, it's a win win situation.
PROS: Will get you sightseeing and earning money at the same time.
CONS: It won't be your holiday, you will have responsibility concerning insurance, food, accommodation, security and safety.

45. Create a subscription website.
A lot of content rich sites on the internet now offer both free and paid membership because specialised content is a hot item.
A subscription site can reap rewards if you provide specialised content, or have a specialist niche in the market.

46. Clean other peoples houses.
Create and print off some leaflets and hand them out. Post through letterboxes saying what you offer, the prices you charge etc... and don't forget to include a contact name and number. You could offer full house cleaning services, or why not offer your services by the hour, for example 1 hours cleaning for £10.00.
PROS: Always a popular service, with most homeowners.
CONS: You will have to get your hands dirty.

47. Clean local offices

This is nearly the same as cleaning people's houses, except with businesses. You could try and get in touch with the business owner, and try and get a contract to do regular office/shop cleaning. Build up your reputation and contacts through word of mouth, and flyers.

48. Offer an Ironing service.

You could do this from you home or go mobile. What about Charging £2 + per piece of ironing you do, or charge people dependant on the weight of the washing, say £10 per bin bag of clothes. Use a method you feel the most comfortable with, write down how and what you will charge then advertise in your local press.

TOP TIP: Advertise at your local universities and colleges.

49. Become a virtual secretary/assistant.

Just like being an office secretary but you will be offering and providing your services on the internet, instead of in a physical location. You could provide administrative assistance for companies and businesses and undertake tasks such as: budgeting and updating accounts. Contact small start-up companies who perhaps don't yet have a physical location but need help with day to day secretarial tasks, advertise on the internet, and maybe advertise at local business centres/agencies. You could charge an hourly daily or task based rate, or even be hired permanently by just one company.

PROS: Offers flexible working and earning.

CONS: Lack of physical contact/communication with others.

50. Gardening, why not become a gardener.

If you are a bit green fingered than this idea could suit you down to the ground. If you have no formal training and would like some why not take a course at your college. You could advertise on notice/bulletin boards and through word of mouth in your local area. Ideally start off with a 15 mile radius. Place adverts in your local classifieds and newspapers.

PROS: You can see the fruits of your labour. Opportunities are arising due to people working more, therefore having less time to attend to their neglected gardens.

CONS: May be a seasonal money making opportunity, dependant on the type of gardening you are doing.

51. Window cleaning.

Offer your services to both individuals and businesses, advertise in your local paper, include a telephone number, contact name and rates you offer. Hand out leaflets and drop these door to door to drum up some business.

PROS: Easy to start up with potentially low advertising costs.

CONS: Work in all weather.

52. Be an Exercise companion.

53. Start a House clearance service.

Place adverts in your local papers and at local community centres saying you offer a free collection, house clearance service, you can then either sell the contents of the house onto a car booter, market trader or second hand shop, or you could try selling the items yourself, for example on a well known auction website.

54.Teach people how to use computers.
Offer local classes at community centres, or offer one to one sessions. Perhaps you could even create a mini How to booklet, e.g. you could produce and sell a how to use word, or excel to the people who you teach, which you could sell at the end of a class. Advertise in your local classifieds/newspaper, offer specials for example 7 lessons for the price of 5, or something similar.

55. Offer to do peoples weekly food/grocery shopping.
This is a service that can cater to everyone, from the young to the old so potentially you have a large target audience. Advertise in newspapers and perhaps at local supermarkets. You could charge people say £5.00 per shop you do for them and do 2 peoples shopping at once to make even more.
TOP TIP: Do online shopping, saves you really leaving the house, and could offer additional discounts.

56. Be a Telephone canvasser, work in canvassing, generating sales for multiple companies/businesses.

57. Organise peoples homes and offices.
Are you organised, if so why not become a professional organiser. You could charge people by the hour, or by the room. Advertise in your local media, through word of mouth and on the internet.
TOP TIP: As an additional service you could perhaps sell storage facilities to your customers, to ensure they keep their places organised.

58. Tutor Children.
Perhaps you are a qualified teacher and wish to supplement your income. Or perhaps you want to tutor children in other areas of their life, apart from education, for example you could tutor children on how to save money or how to keep safe on the internet. A lot of parents will be grateful for your knowledge and a different perspective as most children don't or wont listen to their parents, but may just listen to you.   Its probably best to undertake a CRB check as more people will probably hire you if you can be trusted etc.
PROS: Many parents don't have the time to tutor their children, either educationally or with life's little lessons.
CONS: You have to like children, and you have to be patient.

59. Create and sell handmade jewellery.
Sell your work from a market stall or sell your products on the internet. An online shop is quick and quite affordable to create and can house all of your various projects/products for sale under one roof.
TOP TIP: Offer a custom/made to order service.

60. Source, buy and sell vintage clothing/costumes.
You could buy these products and items online, from auction sites, from second hand/ charity shops and from markets. Sell onto shops or directly onto clients/customers. Advertise through word of mouth and in your local media.

61. Buy and sell restored furniture.
Why not buy old furniture from car boots, scrap yards, house clearances, online auctions etc. Paint, recover, or do whatever needs doing to the item of furniture and then sell on at a profit.

62. Become a proof-reader.

Offer a proofreading service, perhaps to both small businesses and individuals. Start and run this service from your home, and advertise in your local press and media.

TOP TIP: In addition to the above, why not offer your services to self publishers, newsletters, magazines, weekly's.

63. Offer a Garage sale/house sale organiser service.

64. Offer a clothing repair service/alterations service.

Do this from your home and charge per piece. Patience is required to deal with customers, but you could get regular work mending/altering anything from dresses to home furnishings. You could work part-time from home or set up a full time business, advertise locally and get your customers to spread the word about the services you offer. Get extra work by offering your services to curtain stores, clothing shops, dry cleaners, as well as advertising in laundrettes, local post offices, door to door leafleting etc.

65. Washing service.

If you have a washing machine, why not offer to do other peoples washing and again charge them per piece/s or by the weight. Advertise in your local paper, provide a telephone number, along with rates.

TOP TIP: Try advertising at your local university and you may soon see how muck can be turned into money. You could also possibly cross promote or link your washing service into an additional ironing service.

66. Sell sheet music by mail order or through an online shop and so on.

67. Scrapbook for people.
You could help individuals and families organise their photos, their history etc, and you can help businesses organise articles, press releases, photos etc. This service could be applicable to both individuals and businesses. You could charge by the hour.

68. Make and sell children's and adults fancy dress costumes.
Even if your not a dab hand at sewing, why not buy the patterns and get a seamstress to make up the costumes which you can then sell at a profit. Advertise at/with local events organisers and through your local press and media.
PROS: Its creative and artistic and fun.
CONS: Outfits or costumes might be seasonal and so too might be business.

69. Teach people how to use digital cameras.
You could hold classes or teach them in their own homes, help people, tell and show them how to use a digital camera, how to upload pictures to the computer etc. An additional service you could offer could be you could help them pick out and buy a camera that will suit their needs and requirements (for a fee of course).
TOP TIP: Advertise at your local community centres/halls and in your local press/media.

70. Teach people how to use camcorders.
You could hold local classes for example, advertise at local colleges, adult learning centres, night classes etc.

71. Promote others people businesses, seminars or courses.

72. Offer to organise people's home/office/leisure timetables.

Some people need help sorting out their timetables, meetings and work schedules, how much time they have free and when. Why not be this person and get paid at the same time.

PROS: You are providing a very useful, interesting and normally in demand service, especially in cities.

CONS: May get a bit repetitive and perhaps boring, organising others lives.

73. Sell your unwanted items.

For a quick way to get some cash have a sort out, sell stuff that hasn't been used or will not be used in the near future on auction sites (such as eBay). Have a car boot or sell them in your local classifieds paper.

PROS: An easier way to get rid of your clutter, and unwanted items, and turn items into cash.

CONS: Items may not always sell the first time round, this exercise of de cluttering and selling might be a little bit time consuming.

74. Organise specialist sales events.

You could for example hold and organise children's toys and games fairs. Hold sales in local farmers fields, a village halls and community centres.

Charge sellers for tables/stalls/pitches etc, and charge people an entrance/admittance fee, (like a car boot). You will make money once the location rental has been paid off. People are always looking for a bargain, you could hold these at you local village hall/community centre.

TOP TIP: Advertise in your local media and press, and through word of mouth.

75. Organise children's birthday parties.

Sometimes parents don't have the time or the patience to do it themselves, so why not take the hassle off their shoulders. Organise the equipment hire, the location, the cake making and decorating, party bags, invitations and anything else the parents may want.

TOP TIP: Why not write a booklet that gives suppliers of all the products you provided at the party for example, and sell alongside your services = double money.

76. Grow and sell your own fruit and vegetables.

Are you green fingered? If so then this could be a nice little earner for you. You could sell your fresh produce at a local market, or sell to local shops/supermarkets, (check with your council to see what health/food regulations apply first).

PROS: You can see the fruit of you labour, and get paid for it. People love nothing more than home grown food produce.

CONS: The weather may damage some crop, and crop/produce may not turn out as desired.

77. Learn how to value small businesses , and then give independent valuations.

78. Provide a landscape gardener service.

Perhaps you don't want to be a Gardner, fair enough, but are you creative? If so, why not design gardens and then pay somebody else to do the labour. If you don't have a good knowledge of plants, lawn care and a flair for creating and designing gardens then you could think of taking a course for example at you local college.

79. Train to be an interior designer.
Perhaps you are not interested in gardens, how about turning your hand to interior design, get qualified with a distance learning course and then work freelance, set up a consultancy and offer interior design consultations for both the home and the workplace.
TOP TIP: Offer a free consultation, to get more paying clients.

80. Learn a new skill or subject.
What is missing in your local area/community, is it a gap you could fill, if so why not get the skills and experience necessary and then put it to use by either teaching it to somebody else for a fee, or getting a second job with your new added skill/qualification. You could for example learn Italian and then teach people or small groups Italian for their holidays.
PROS: You can learn a new skill.
CONS: May take a bit of time to start making money, as you have to learn before you can earn.

81. Make and sell greeting cards.
From birthday cards to Christmas cards, you can sell your designs individually either direct through mail order, or online. Or as wholesale to local shops and retailers.
TOP TIP: If you are a dab hand at making cards then why not hold card marking classes/courses, to supplement your income from selling handmade cards.

82. Can you speak another language? If not then learn a second language.
Languages are becoming increasing popular and in demand so why not fill this need and become a language tutor. You could teach individuals or small businesses for example, your new found knowledge.
TOP TIP: See where the demand lies for languages, why not do a bit of market research to see the what the most popular language to learn is.

83. Why not start your Own Home Shopping Show.

You could do this for example over the internet, using you Webcam.

84. Train to be a photographer.

If you are not already one of course, you could take evening classes, study full time, or get a job as a photographer's assistant and learn first hand, get on the job experience.

PROS: You could specialise in different types of photography.

CONS: You will have to build up a reputation, of being on time, fair with your pricing, and excellent in your quality and standards of work.

85. Organise/Hold weight loss classes.

Perhaps you could target your local area. Why not contact weight watchers for example and become a representative.

TOP TIP: Why not sell weight loss products/fitness classes etc alongside your weight watching programmes, to increase your income.

86. Become a freelance writer.

You could cover multiple subjects and topics, from travel to sport. Perhaps you could write content for online directories/websites, or even local newspapers.

TOP TIP: Consider studying journalism, and choose what topics you want to write about, then find your target market, write articles and stories until you get noticed.

87. Specialise in fitting CCTV security cameras .

Security cameras are everywhere, but there's still businesses and homes that don't have them. For equipment, check the exchange & Mart and trade magazines. Advertise in your local press and media.

TOP TIP: Market your services and products to both businesses and private individuals.

88. Sell lucky charms.

Everyone loves a good luck charm and items that bring luck, so why not cater to their needs and wants. People want charms that represent love, happiness, luck etc. You could sell products from horseshoes to 4 leaf clovers.

PROS: This is a niche all on its own.

CONS: You might not be able to satisfy everyone's demands for their own lucky charm.

89. Self-Improvement Classes .

Offer Self-Improvement Classes. Teach people what you know about losing weight, getting back your confidence and so on.

90. Get paid to promote other peoples businesses.

Why not promote peoples businesses and service on behalf of them for fixed rates. You could drum up new business for them and take a healthy commission in return.

TOP TIP: Target new local small businesses, and remember you don't have to advertise just one business/service.

91. Buyers Guide.

How about writing, publishing and selling a guide to the best prices available in your area, where to buy etc. As your Buyers Guides popularity increases, charge more for businesses that wish to list their product/service. You could sell the guide for at least £5.00 as people are always willing to pay money in the short term if it means they can make savings in the long term.

PROS: Potential is limitless and endless, for example you don't have to only cover your local area. New businesses seem to always be opening, so advertise your guide to these and possible their customers/employees.

CONS: Will involve PR, advertising and sales, and lots of it, if you want your guide packed with useful information.

92. Start a Lonely Hearts club.

How about starting your own lonely hearts club, you could advertise for, list and match names of people who would like to meet others. Go on their ages, hobbies and interests. What do they like and look for in others, for example religion, interests, education etc. Arrange mystery dates and charge each side for your service.

TOP TIP: Why not place adverts in your local press, radio, papers/media.

93. Moving day assistant.

Help people with this stressful process. Print up cards announcing your willingness to pack removal vans; help people pack up their belongings (and possibly sell them packaging materials at the same time). Advertise your services in your local paper/classifieds.

TOP TIP: Advertise at storage facilities, estate agencies etc.

94. Start a credit control service/business.

95. How about being a Business broker.

A Business broker matches buyers and sellers of both small and medium-size businesses. Your main aim is to save buyers and business owners money, help them to avoid mistakes, and market the seller's business. You will oversee the whole business buying and selling process, ensuring all transactions are completed smoothly and efficiently. You can make money by charging both buyers and sellers fees.

96. Offer a service that fits security locks onto doors and windows.

You could buy locks from wholesalers and advertise in your local press. Get in with window fitters, conservatory specialists/companies etc to see if you can collaborate with them, this will offer you the chance to expand your service/s and building a positive reputation.

97. Start a dating club for just women, or just men.

98. Property.
There are lot of ways to make money in property including: buy to let, buying to sell on. Changing the properties use, buying houses below market value and selling on and by improving, refurbishing, repairing and then selling.
TOP TIP: Why not form a partnership with someone else going into property, therefore splitting the costs, and maybe the stress as well.

99.Donate Plasma.

100. Computer Cleaning.
If you are computer savvy, charge a small fee for cleaning up slow running computers. You could update slow programs, delete old, unwanted and unused programmes etc. Sell your services through in local classified/newspapers as well as selling door to door, leafleting drops for example to advertise your services to older computer users could prove popular.
PROS: More and more people have computers, and so you could build up a regular supply of work, especially through word of mouth.
CONS: Find out what data protection acts you may need to follow, as you may be viewing personal files, information etc.

Chapter 2 –How to Create Multiple Income Streams

What are Multiple Income streams?

Multiple Income streams are multiple ways of earning money, an example of an income stream could be earning money through selling a product or service you have not made, created or produced yourself (know as being an affiliate). Another income stream could be something like having a part time job.

To create multiple income streams successfully you need to be focused, motivated and disciplined.

Don't spread yourself too thin. Money will come in faster and you will achieve better results if you stay focused.

Focus on one project until this project is earning money. Once success is achieved, move onto another idea, which will in turn become a new income stream. This is how multiple income streams are built, you cannot build Multiple income streams in one day or even overnight. You have to focus on one project at a time, get it up and running and earning, then move onto the next idea/money making opportunity.

To effectively create multiple income streams your first task is to create a mind map of all of your ideas, and see which idea is appropriate for you at that time (which idea you can turn into money).

You have to treat each idea as a business. You have to be able to enjoy each new idea, have the time and ability to develop each idea, as well as retain passion for each idea/business, even after it has started earning you money.

Each money making idea/opportunity must be maintained, think of it a bit like a flower, if you do not keep watering and taking care of the flower it will not continue to grow and flourish.

You cannot forget about or abandon you money making idea/income stream after it has started earning you money, because if you stop working on it, then it will not develop, and your income stream will cease to operate, hence the money will stop coming in, and you will have to start again from the beginning.

Some ideas for multiple streams of income include selling e-books, earning money through your website, or selling affiliate programs. Any single idea in this book can be turned into a multiple income stream, add this to ideas you may think of, or come up with while reading and working through this book and you will see the potential to earn money is endless.

Below are a few possible multiple income streams, you might want to start.

1. Sell used books.

2. Start a blog.

3. Become a tutor.

4. Start a website.

5. Sell e-Books.

6. Write articles.

7. Get a part-time job.

8. Start a paid subscription website.

Remember that whatever idea you choose you must stick with it. You will find that once your first Income stream is in place, the others will not be as difficult as your first thought.
Each idea needs to be taken seriously, it needs to be planned and executed. Patience is required for each idea you wish to turn into an Income stream as success does not happen, and will not happen overnight.
Remember to research each new idea as you don't want to waste any time or money on trying ideas that aren't going to work for you in the long run.

When considering a new Multiple Income stream consider

• What steps you will need to take in order for it to be a success.

• Its pros and cons, what advantages and disadvantages does it have, for example a pro might be that it has low start up costs.

• Are you genuinely interested in the ideas, as if you aren't it will not succeed. You have to do something because you have a genuine interest in it, not just for the money.

• How many hours a day/week you will need to dedicate to the new Income stream, as well as the additional hours you will have to spend maintaining current income streams.

Remember the trick to successfully building Multiple Income streams is to never work on more that one idea/business at once. Get each Income stream up, running and earning before considering another one. It is better to have two successful income streams as apposed to five or six failing income streams. With each idea/income stream it is useful to have a timetable or schedule, which allows you to divide and manage your time more effectively.

If you create a schedule and stick to it, you idea/income stream is more likely to be successful.

Below is an example for a new idea/potential Income stream.

Week One: Research the idea.

Week Two: Research the ideas pros and cons.

Week Three: What are the start up costs, is it viable?

Week Four: How much money can I make?

Remember that both mind maps and timetables are also useful motivation tactics, for example when you feel tired and perhaps a bit bored with an idea, and maybe you feel it is going nowhere, refer back to your timetable, or your mind map for that money making idea, see how far you have come, and how far the idea has developed. Evaluate the idea again to see if it is worth progressing with and also remember that if an idea is not worth progressing with, it is not the end of the world. You have still learnt more about ways to make money, and who knows the experience may come in handy for another money making idea.

THE 4 STEPS TO SUCCESSFULLY CREATING MULTIPLE INCOME STREAMS

STEP 1 - Give each of your ideas life, allow the idea to develop, analyse it, work out its pros and cons, work out if you used it how long it would take to be a profitable idea. Jot down all of your thoughts and feelings about the idea, including gut feelings and intuition.

STEP 2 – Create a timetable for each idea, give everything a time and a place, manage your time effectively and you will see the results. Prioritise tasks, and remember that creating a timetable for an idea/income stream is just the same as creating your timetable for success. If you fail to plan, you plan to fail.

STEP 3 – Maintain, Grow and Evaluate each and every income stream. An Income stream will not grow or develop on its own, for example a website cannot maintain itself, it cannot update articles, programs and web pages without your help, just the same applies to an Income stream. It cannot make money without you maintaining it, evaluating the idea at every stage. Creating a growth and maintenance timetable will help ensure its success, growth and development.

STEP 4 – MOVE ON. Once you have one idea under control, and you have planned for its growth, development, and maintenance then move onto creating your next income stream. Perhaps you might want to use your first income stream as the basis for your future income streams.

THE BENEFITS OF CREATING MULTIPLE INCOME STREAMS

• You can create your own income.

• You can make more free time for yourself and your family.

• You can work more flexible working hours; forget the 9-5.

• Income streams can be both online and offline.

TOP TIPS TO HELP YOUR MULTIPLE INCOME STREAMS SUCCEED

• Jot down and diversify all of your thoughts and ideas.
• Don't be negative, negative thoughts stop positive thinking.
• Schedule in breaks and *me time*. Regular rest also gives you free thinking time and allows you to re-energise your batteries ready for more money making.
• Remember large budgets are not usually required to start new income streams, start small and build each income stream up.

HOW LONG WILL IT TAKE UNTIL I SEE THE PROFITS

This depends on your ideas, but a usual idea for example selling e-books or becoming an affiliate marketer is outlined below:

0-3 months is the time usually require for researching your idea, finding out its pros and cons, market research, product research etc.

4-6 months when starting the income stream building up its income through reputation, trust and advertising/promotion.

6-9 months usually when you start to see the money, this is the time when you know your market. You know what the market is lacking, you know how to research the market, find out what it needs, and how much money you can make on your products/services.

Remember that each idea is unique and so the time taken to make it profitable will vary, don't let this put you off, as the rewards reaped may well be worth the extra time taken in the areas of planning and researching.

Chapter 3 – Ways to make money 101 - 200

101. Sell home made products.
Check with your local council about what regulations may be in place with regards to selling hand made products such as soaps, gels, crèmes etc. You could sell your items through local shops, boutiques, on the internet and by mail order.
TOP TIP: Research your market; find out what people want and what prices they are willing to pay.

**102. Start a service that offers help to
people to construct their flat pack furnitur**e.
A lot of people don't have the time or the patience to assemble the furniture. Why not do it for them, take away the hassle and charge them a fee, either based by the hour or number of pieces of furniture you put together.
PROS: More people are buying flat pack furniture, this is a large target market.
CONS: You have to be patient.

**103. How about keeping fit and getting paid, why not
join the TA or the Army.**

104. Motivate People.
You are obviously motivated to make more money or else you wouldn't be reading this book, so why not pass on your knowledge of motivation to someone else(for a fee of course). There are opportunities for motivation courses, lessons or booklets. You could provide and present your material in house for/to companies, or what about perhaps offering one to one sessions for individuals, you could even organise local community motivation classes. Whatever you feel
The most comfortable in and wherever there is the greatest demand.
TOP TIP: Research what motivates people, what are their motivators.

105. Be a Focus group organiser.

106. Offer to do errands/services for the older generation.

Such as shopping, picking up medical prescriptions, paying bills etc, offer to do this for a fee.

TOP TIP: Why not offer this alongside a companion service, or why not get a few elderly clients whose errands you can do on the same day to cut your costs and increase your profit.

107. Sell houses for people.

Provide an offer people can't refuse, especially in today's market. Tell people you want to have 14 days to try and sell their house. Don't charge high commissions like estate agents and you should be able to make a nice tidy sum on each property you sell. Utilise property sale websites, and free Trials. Remember to seek professional advice before signing or agreeing to anything. Read up on buying and selling laws and regulations, and if you choose to follow this money making opportunity you should be successfully earning in no time.

PROS: Very good service to offer, when perhaps house sales are slow.

CONS: Could take longer than initially thought to sell a property.

108. Organise/host adult only parties.

Why not host adult parties? This is an ideal weekend or evening money-maker that can be very profitable and fun to run. Send for a number of catalogues and price lists from various suppliers to compare products and prices. Compile a list of the best items and purchase a small stock of each one, using one of each for demonstration purposes. Hand out brochures and order forms at the party and use a friend to demonstrate the goods.

PROS: Flexible working, easy to organise and promote.

CONS: You may want to buy the products for yourself, hence make no money.

41

109. Offer a pet grooming service.

How about offering a mobile service, dog grooming is now considered a necessity and is almost essential for all dog/pet owners. You will need to be fairly good at using a pair of scissors and hair clippers. Some dogs may need expert handling/grooming. Learn as much as you can before setting up on your own. Offer nail clipping as a freebie to get your business/service going. Or perhaps you could offer a free dog wash and dry for every friend that an existing client refers to your, for example.

PROS: This business can be run from home or mobile.

CONS: Not recommended if you are allergic to dogs. You will need to be patient as not all animals enjoy or want to be groomed.

110. Why not be a car phone fitter.

111. Draw/paint/collage.

How about making your own works of art and selling them yourself. Who knows you might be the next Picasso. Sell your work direct, through an online shop/website, or perhaps even an art gallery/exhibition. Hold your own events and sell your own artwork alongside others to generate a buzz and some extra cash.

TOP TIP: Why not get other artists work exhibited and charge them a fee at the same time.

112. Be a drunk drive assist.

Help people get home after a night out.

113. Join Market research panels.

Online, face to face or through survey panels, join local market research panels/companies, search the internet for panels and market researchers in your area.

114. Offer an Errand Service.
Target families and business people, who may not have enough hours in the day. This money making opportunity can fit in with your own life and errands and has the advantage of virtually no overheads.
TOP TIP: Place adverts in your local paper/press.

115. Manicurist/Pedicurist.
Train to be a manicurist/pedicurist and go mobile. Build up a reliable clientele, training costs can be kept low by studying at your local college and you could also train to do nail extensions. You could also set up within other local service providers such as hairdressers.
TOP TIP: You don't have to do nails yourself, you could hire the work out (hire a nail technician).

116. Mystery Shopping.
Sign up with mystery shopping websites/companies and you will get paid to shop. Sometimes you can also keep the items you bought while you were *working*. Visit and discussion forums to find out which companies and types of jobs will suit you and your circumstances.

117. Why not be a balloonist.

118. Become a TV extra or a film extra.
Be on TV and get paid for it, you can search for opportunities on the internet and in your local press and media.
TOP TIPS: Learn tricks, showcase your talent and be nice to everyone to get you noticed, don't burn any bridges.

119. Do deliveries for local shops and businesses.
Having a car is essential, but you could get you transport
costs paid and then get paid per delivery you complete
etc...for example work for a local takeaway.
Contact your local shops, stores and takeaways and sell your
delivery services, charge them per delivery you make and try
to work for multiple businesses to reduce your costs and
increase your profit.

**120. Start a business/service arranging internships and
work placements for students.**

121. Provide storytelling at local schools and nurseries.
You could read to children before/after school, and charge
parents perhaps £1.00 per child or so every story telling
session they attend, make storytelling more exciting and
interactive, get the children and possibly parents involved
TOP TIP: Why not offer story writing classes alongside
storytelling, perhaps marketed/aimed towards parents.

122. Create and sell your own information products.
Why not create your own how to guides or information CDs,
and sell online, by direct mail/mail order or as wholesale to
other retailers.
TOP TIP: Find out what people want to learn, or improve
about themselves, then market it and away you go.

123. Why not be a Relocation agent.

124. Teach people how to save money and how to budget.

How about holding money saving classes, teach people how to tighten their belts, and how to use money saving comparison sites such as www.pricerunner.com.

PROS: You will help keep people financially sound, and help them appreciate and make more of what they have.

CONS: You have to be money wise and money savvy, you have to be up to date on the latest accounts, savings etc, to help people get the best deals around.

125. Start a Bill reminder service.

126. Organise Christmas/seasonal events.

This could be for anything from gatherings for families or office parties for businesses, open a seasonal business that doesn't require a physical location/office. This is just like a party organising/event organising business but more specialised and seasonal.

127. Hold money making classes.

How about putting your knowledge and experience into action and hold either a series of money making classes, either charged per session or per block of sessions/classes.

TOP TIP: Why not take along your copy of 1001 ways to make money, or buy a few copies to sell on.

128. Buy and sell celebrity autographed merchandise and items.

Anything from football merchandise to pop stars merchandise. Remember the amount of profit you make will depend on the popularity of the celebrity (past present or future).

TOP TIP: Make sure all your merchandise is legitimate, don't buy or sell fakes or copies.

129. Be an Animal behaviourist/psychologist.

130. Buy a commercial or a residential property with a buy to let mortgage.

You could let the house/property out over a period of say 5 years+ and see how well it is going. Remember to make sure your rent covers your initial costs/mortgage, then anything on top = profit, hence making money.

PROS: What is the saying *as safe as houses*

CONS: Large initial outlet, its not a get rich quick scheme.

131. Be an energy consultant for multiple suppliers.

132. Offer to source new clients for businesses.

Both start-up businesses and established businesses are always looking for new customers/clients, and what better way to earn money than by utilising your contacts and acquaintances, earn a commission for all of your hard work and effort. You could build and sell customer mailing lists, or perhaps just refers people/contacts you know to the business, and take a commission from any sales.

133. Become a researcher/intermediary for anything.

Do you know one person that is perhaps searching for a Car to buy, and perhaps you know another person who is looking for a buyer for their car, if so, why not be the connexion between the two parties, become the middle man and earn a commission/introduction fee from both side/ both parties.

TOP TIP: Advertise in your local paper, through word of mouth and networking and so on.

134. Why not Open a café press store online.

135. Pen your knowledge and experiences.
How about putting pen to paper and write a book, you can get it self published and sell it yourself, the costs and overheads are low and if you have a different book/story profits can be soon made, someone is always interested in somebody else's life/history.

136. Create a niche blog.
A blog is an online web log, like a diary, where you add online entries, you can make money on your blog by adding features such as Google ad sense. A good place to start researching your blog, and what you want to write about is
www.blogger.com – where you can create a free blog.
PROS: Most blogs are free to set up, and you can get paid to type your thoughts, daily goings on etc
CONS: Remembering to regularly update your blog, keep it fresh and interesting.

137. Start a press cutting service.

138. Help local businesses.
You could for example provide services from your home such as data entry, typing, answering service, help small businesses grown, expand etc.
TOP TIP: Advertise in your local business centres.

139. Help people to write or create a CV/Resume.
Hold CV/Resume writing classes for example at you local jobcentre. Or why not hold one to one sessions, charge per CV you create or perhaps per hour spent on helping and creating a CV with someone.

140. Offer a service painting or creosoting wooden fences.

141. Join online cash back and rewards sites.
Did you know that you can earn money completing offers and
daily clicks, an example of one of these sites is:
www.quidco.com.
You can earn money back when you shop or even complete
free trial offers. To find a full list of cash back sites you should
join up for to make even more money please visit the Useful
Contacts/Website chapter at the end of this book.

**142. Buy and sell items in bulk from wholesalers and
sell individually.**
Sell directly to customers through your chosen sales channels,
for example online, through mail order. The advantage of this
is you can have higher profit margins, and sell almost
anything that you have bought wholesale, examples of
products you could sell include: clothes, cosmetics, phone
accessories.
TOP TIP: Make sure you buy products that can be individually
sold.

143. Modelling.
Fancy becoming a model, why not become a (parts model),
for example a hair model, hand model, foot model etc.
Modelling has opportunities for everyone of all shapes and
sizes, contact modelling agencies in your surrounding areas
and see what they can offer you.
PROS: Models are always required.
CONS: Remember not all offers/jobs are genuine. Also
remember never to pay any money up front to join so called
modelling agencies.

**144. Start a snack run on local industrial and business
estates.**

145. Offer to deliver leaflets (flyers) for local Companies/businesses.

Keep fit and earn money at the same time, for example place an advert in your local paper, and say you are willing to post door to door leaflets, sales letters etc. Include your name, a contact number and price/rate you charge per piece of material delivered.

TOP TIP: Perhaps you could also arrange a sales/commission fee with the company, whereby if you create a sale or sales lead from handing out material you should receive a set commission.

146. Playing computer games.

Why not become a games tester, search the internet for more information and current opportunities. Contact games manufacturers and ask them if they require any games testers, or be a games tester for a computer gaming magazine.

PROS: Paid to play.

CONS: May only be a temporary job/work contract. If it looks too good to be true it probably is.

147. Teach people your skills and knowledge.

Do you know how to sew, if so why not advertise local sewing classes. Do you know how to knit, if so teach people to knit and so on.

TOP TIP: You don't just have to teach through classes, why not teach online, through a website, a CD, a book or even a guide.

148. Why not be a mobile bartender.

149. Buy and sell second hand items on auction Websites and through your local free classified papers. Buy items from second hand shops or from people who are having clearances, or even at car boots if you want.

PROS: Low start up costs.

CONS: Finding good quality used items can sometimes be quite time consuming, the best way to get over this is to allocate yourself a set period of time to find/source items.

150. Stooze.
Another way to some extra money is by stoozing – stoozing is a way of making money on your credit cards. It is a ways of transferring money from your card into savings accounts, and earning interest on the cards *free money* for more information visit the very up to date and informative website www.stoozing.com.

PROS: Virtually free money.

CONS: You need to be very organised.

151. How about being a master of ceremonies.

152. Be a ghost writer.
Don't fancy writing and releasing work under your own name, how about being a ghost writer then? This is someone who for example writes autobiographies for celebrities who perhaps cannot write down what they feel, or for perhaps politicians who need to write letters or maybe even autobiographies. Why not get in touch with local publishing houses to see if they can provide further information/tips on how you can become a ghost-writer.

153. Start matched betting.
Make money by using and utilising free bets from online bookies and gambling websites.

154. Create computer generate quizzes and games.

155. Teach DIY.
If you're a hands on handy person why not teach your tricks etc to people of all ages. You could Hold DIY classes on a Saturday, advertise in local papers and say charge £5 per person per class they attend.

156. Create and sell gift baskets/hampers.
Baskets and hampers can be made for all occasions from births to birthdays and weddings. You could sell these directly onto customers, or, you could sell them as wholesale (supply wholesale to shops and businesses) or sell them local retail shops/gift shops/card shops/event organisers.
TOP TIP: Offer a customisation service, for example where people get to choose what they put in each hamper, and what hamper products are put into.

157. How about offering a vacuum cleaning and possible repair service.

158. Create a weekend business.
You could for example supplement your income by starting a weekend lawn mowing business, or even a car washing business/service.

159. Customise and sell women's and children's shoes.
You could buy a few pairs of shoes from wholesalers and customise the shoes with ribbons, beads, sequins, buttons, charms and whatever else tickles your fancy. Remember people will pay more to have customised and hand made items, plus if you wanted you could offer a design your own shoes service to really get people talking.
PROS: You get to be creative.
CONS: You will have to advertise, and build up trust and confidence right from the start, with your products.

160. Got a spare room/bedroom in your house.
If so why not rent it out to students, or professionals either charging daily weekly or monthly rent.
TOP TIP: Advertise at your local colleges/universities.

161. Provide Post natal care.

162. Blast from the past, sell 50s 60s 70s etc memorabilia/items/artefacts.
Items from the past are currently in fashion, everything makes a comeback, and if you wanted you could specialise in one era, and create your own niche. You could sell through a wide variety of sales channels from online auctions to having your own website.

163. Design and sell customised clothing.
You could design to make, or design to order. Offer a unique customising service. Always remember that if you don't feel confident enough or perhaps you don't have the time to customise the pieces yourself, take them along with the pattern to a seamstress/dressmaker (but remember when creating a price to include time taken/materials used).
TOP TIP: Build up a good reputation for quality and price, always ask for customer feedback.

164. Sell your hair.
If you have long hair, get it cut off and sell it to companies who will turn your hair into someone else's hair extensions.

165. How about offering a telephone answering service.

166. Become a floral arranger.
Create and sell floral arrangements, from weddings to christenings or parties. Use combinations of fresh and silk flowers to get unique results.
TOP TIP: Get in contact with local events organisers to tell them about your service.

167. Make and sell handmade invitations.
For all types of events, from christening invitations to wedding
Invitations. You could sell your invitations in boutiques, shops
catering to the type of invitation you produce, for example
Christening invitations to baby shops etc.

168. Start a tennis academy.

169. Become a personal trainer/personal fitness coach.
More people have less time to work out, and so this is the
perfect money making opportunity, as you can keep fit
alongside earning money. You could work with individuals on
a one to one basis, or perhaps offer one hour lunch break
classes to local businesses.
PROS: You will get paid to keep fit.
CONS: You will have to be constantly motivated, and always
have a smile on your face, as if your not happy, people will
pick up on your negative attitude.

**170. Invent something or just improve an existing
Product.**
Think of something that would make everyday life that little
bit easier, or why not write your ideas down and then sell
them.
TOP TIP: Look at what there is in the current market, what
could be bigger, faster, stronger etc.

**171. Why not become a Bookseller, perhaps selling door
to door.**

172. Become a steward at your local football ground.
This is a great money making opportunity because its usually
cash in hand and its only for 2 hours plus. Contact your local
football clubs and see if they need an extra hand.

173. Buy and sell customised one off handbags, shoes and earrings.
Every woman loves handbags and shoes, and especially when they match, you could import/export shoes/handbags from Spain and Italy. Customise pieces and then sell them on directly, through wholesale, through local retailers, or offer home parties to sell all of your products in one go.
TOP TIP: Why not focus on importing products from all over the world.

174. Start a millionaires dating club.
For example offer a service for millionaires who are looking for a date/escort etc.

175. Open a coffee shop/stall.
If you are near to a university, or college, even better! People enjoy a cup of coffee before work/university etc, and sometimes afterwards as well, get a regular customer base and your profits will soon mount up expect anything from £1.00 profit per cup of coffee, and if you need any more motivation just take a look at how successful some of the bigger well known brands have been.

176. Record and sell your own music.
Establish yourself on line, create a webpage, get music CDs made and then sell them yourself.

177. Write and Sell poetry.
This could be your own work, or perhaps yours and others work. You could hold poetry readings, workshops, and maybe even writing classes.
TOP TIP: Sell your poetry to magazines, books, weeklies.

178. Make your own competitions and quizzes and sell Them to magazines.
There's a lot of newspapers and magazines which print crosswords for their readers. Some puzzle magazines are filled with them. Sell your quizzes and crosswords to make it worthwhile. Check the internet for sources and ensure you retain some form of copyright on your works as you can then resell them to other magazines and publications.

179. Start an eBay business.

180. Become a professional competition entrant.
You could enter competitions for living, ones to win money, or prizes (which you may be able to sell on for money).
TOP TIP: There are lots of useful online source, concerning where you can apply for competitions, deadlines, entry fees (if applicable) etc. Write down and keep a not of each competition you enter.

181. Sell products handmade or hand decorated by Children.
This could include mugs, towels etc anything parents and family members/friends will cherish.
TOP TIP: Advertise your services through school's playgroups and nurseries.

182. Start a pond maintenance service.

183. Design greetings cards to sell online and offline.
If you're artistic design a range of greeting cards you can sell online could easily produce a useful source of income. Using a PC and a good quality printer, a variety of designs could be produced based around popular themes. You could also offer a personalised design service. Each design could be adapted to use the name of the buyer.

184. Buy and sell websites.

Websites that perhaps are an existing business, or websites developed but not yet used. You could sell them on to entrepreneurs, small businesses and even individuals.

PROS: Low cost to start-up and buy websites.

CONS: May take time to find websites that are actually worth buying (that have a resale value).

185. Advertise on your car or mode of transport.

You can get paid to have a companies logo/business name on your car so why not give it a go. Advertise that you have advertising space for sale on your transport, include how many miles/routes you cover each day/week, a contact name and number, plus how much money you want from the advertisers to place the companies advertising on your mode of transport.

TOP TIP: Auction off your advertising space, and donate half of the proceeds to charity.

186. Become an affiliate marketer.

Promote websites/products on behalf of companies and a commission for each referral/customer the company gains through you, get paid based on your performance.

PROS: You can earn some serious money referring Friends and contacts to your affiliate programmes.

CONS: May take a while to build a steady regular income.

187. Become a house sitter.
This would be ideal for people who aren't tied down with property of their own. This involves you living in and looking after other peoples homes. It's for people, who are regularly away from home. It provides security and peace of mind that their property is being looked after and kept in good order. References will be required as proof that people can trust you and rely on you. This will be easier to achieve once you have some experience under your belt.
TOP TIP: You could maybe offer this alongside looking after peoples pets while they are away (pet sitter).

188. Train to become a physiotherapist.

189. Become a pet sitter.
If you like animals why not look after peoples pets in there own homes, for example while they are at work, what could be better you could paid to look after peoples pets but don't have to spend hours cleaning up your own house.
PROS: It is just like babysitting, but with animals
CONS: You have to like animals, and have time for them, and their needs and wants.

190. Start a Bulletin board.
Rent a space where there is heavy pedestrian traffic, in other words where loads of people are walking and will see your ads every day. Sell your advertising space to hotels, shops, cafes, small businesses etc, and all others to whose advantage it is to be listed on your advertising board, build you income by building the number of bulleting/advertising boards you have.

191. Why not be a wholesaler.
Why not buy products in bulk from manufacturers, add a mark up and then sell on say to home party organisers, small start-up businesses and so on.

192. Start up a bookkeeping service.

If you are not a qualified bookkeeper, why not train to be one? There are lots of small businesses who need the services of a good book-keeper. You should be able to keep simple records, balance the books and fill in tax returns for any small businesses or individuals. Check out your local education centres, distance learning courses etc and information on the internet for courses available in book-keeping and what it involves.

PROS: More people are setting up small/medium size businesses, that require bookkeepers.

CONS: You need to be good with numbers and figures.

193. Business Presentation Provider.

Help businesses create presentations whether on computer or on paper, you could offer services such as writing business presentations, organising and planning presentations etc.

194. Brochure designer.

You could design brochures for businesses on your computer, and sell the brochure designs, or you could try designing and printing the brochures from your home computer/PC. Your brochures and products will probably appeal to small and start up businesses as well as individuals and sole traders.

PROS: You get to be creative and work from home.

CONS: You may need to network for work, and start with producing free brochures to show what skills you have.

195. Candle Maker.

You could make and sell candles, sell them in your local area, online, on auction websites, by mail order and even through wholesale to retail outlets/shops.

TOP TIP: Hold candle making parties and classes to further top up your income.

196. Set up a business that rents out quad bikes and other off road vehicles.

197. Audio Books producer.
People don't always have the time or patience to read a book, they would rather listen to information rather than read it. Why not produce audio books, why not create and put your own material onto audio books.
If you don't want to use your own information, why not offer this service to publishers/authors who may require their work turning into audio books.

198. Hold/provide Astrology readings.
If you have a thorough knowledge of all things related to astrology and how people in the various zodiac signs are affected by the stars and planets. Offer free readings to get people interested then get more work through word of mouth, local press and media etc.
TOP TIP: Offer astrology readings for parties, get in touch with event organisers.

199. Start an art/photo restoration service or business.
This involves touching up and restoring pieces back to their original self and glory. Advertise through local press, media, galleries, magazines and through word of mouth. as well as through ancestry magazines, workshops and websites. Advertise that you can restore old family photos, old school photos, or old work photos etc.
PROS: You will never get two projects the same.
CONS: Could be a timely and length process, to learn how to restore photos, and then apply what you have learnt.

200. Make and sell toys for children.
You could for example make soft toys, teddy bears, dolls or even wooden toys. Advertise in parents magazines, at local schools, community halls, nurseries etc.
TOP TIPS: Check with your local council what rules and regulations apply to you making and selling these items/products.

Chapter 4 – How to increase your profits

How to increase your profits

Once you put some of these money making ideas in action, and they are up and running you will probably want to know how you can increase your profits. Here are some top tips and handy hints on how you can go about increasing the profits.

You could: **Increase The Number Of Sales** - Try and sell more of your products, or provide more services.
Reach More People: Getting more people to buy your products/services. This is the most obvious approach to increasing your sales, and it can work, provided your market is not saturated. Get more customers by offering a personal touch if you are providing a service, discounting or providing special offers on your products. Freebies always work well in generating more business/sales.

You could: **Cut your costs** - There are 2 types of costs which affect you when it comes to increasing your profits, you need to consider variable costs which vary depending for example on the volume of orders you process, and fixed costs which are the same regardless of the amount that you sell. For example web hosting.

You could: **Increase the Profit Per Sale -** Try an earn more from each sale that you make. For example sometimes raising the price of an item makes it more attractive to potential customers/clients. Make sure that you are offering value for money. You could try "up-selling". This is when a customer is interested in buying your basic product, offer them a great deal on a more expensive product, or on a bundle of products and services you have on offer. Customers believe they are getting a better deal so will probably but more often than not.

TOP 5 WAYS TO INCREASE YOUR PROFITS

1. Increase the products or services you sell, diversification is essential when it comes to increasing profits.

2. Keep existing customers. Don't spend more money advertising to get new customers, spend a bit of time contacting your previous and existing customers, as it costs more money to find and get new customers than it does to just keep in touch and keep your existing customers.

3. Test your prices. Increase your prices, even by just an extra few percent. Customers normally don't notice, yet you are still providing 100% + customer service and value, it is just costing them a little bit more

4. Continually provide customer satisfaction. Talk to your customers, listen to them and find out what they want and why. Good customer service leads to good word of mouth advertising, which results in more sales and increased profits. Listening and talking to all of your customers = an increase in your profits.

5. Enhance the perceived value of your product, an example of this would be to alter the price of a product dependant on what area you are selling to.

Chapter 5 – Ways to make money 201 – 300

201. Learn how to baby sign and hold regular baby sign Classes.
These classes enable parents to learn how to communicate without words with their babies, it increases the bond between baby and parent.
TOP TIP: Hold weekend workshops, that show parents how to communicate and understand what their baby wants.

202. Hire out scaffolding to small decorating businesses And D.I.Y. enthusiasts.
People need this type of product to carry out exterior painting and maintenance work. Perhaps you could off a free delivery service. Advertise in local newspapers, your local press, the yellow pages and through word of mouth.

203. Learn how to repair clocks and watches.
Why not learn and then start a business repairing these from home. Start a service or business that does watch and jewellery repairs. Specialised courses are available to teach you how to repair jewellery and watches. You could tailor your services to suit jewellers who usually contract out all repair work. You could even open a stall on a market, or perhaps start a stall in your local shopping centre.
PROS: Everyone always requires clock and watch repairs
CONS: You may have to learn and practice a new skill/trade.

204. Sell diet/weight loss products.
You could sell these products through online shops and mail order. Why not advertise at local weight loss classes. You could sell ranges of natural products, detoxification products for example.
TOP TIP: Link up with local diet classes/agents to actively promote each others services and products.

205. Why not train in Homeopathy.

206. Buy and sell second hand cars.
You could buy cars, and then just resell them making a mark up in the process, or you could buy a second hand car, perhaps a classic, and either restore it, or get it professionally restored, then sell at a profit.

TOP TIP: Why not visit a scrap yard and see what gems they are hiding, or try looking at online auctions for bargains.

207. You could be a land searcher.
Work for either estate agencies or for individuals looking for land for sale, or work for both. Search for land that's for sale, charge the buyer your commission fee. You could always find the land and then find a buyer.

PROS: There is always land for sale, and there is always demand. There is lots of money to be made in land and with the commissions it could offer.

CONS: You may have to wait a while for someone to purchase the land you are selling dependant on its location, accessibility etc.

208. Operate a few vending machines.
They are convenient and always there when you need a drink or a snack, so why not get in on the action? They can dispense just about any item like sanitary towels, snacks and chewing gum. It's a great way to make money. It's like having a shop, but of course doesn't't have all the overheads. You will require some investment as you need to purchase the vending machines. You need to undertake market research, to ensure there's a demand for the items you wish to sell.

TOP TIP: Remember location, location, location is essential. Why not buy a second hand vending machine to start with.

209. Sell mobile phone accessories.

You could sell these online, on a market stall, or through mail order? You could if you wanted to also sell ring tones, phone charms, mobile phone holders, SIM cards, and anything else you may be able to think of.

210. Organise walking trips.

This will not cost you anything but it will earn you money and keep you fit. Why not arrange weekly or fortnightly walks. Advertise in your local press and media and away you go. Charge an organisation fee, for example £10 for the day which includes lunch.

TOP TIP: You can cater to a wide variety of people with this service, from schoolchildren to pensioners.

211. Organise hen nights/stag nights.

Source suppliers of cheeky outfits, organise pub and bar crawls, provide a one stop shop for people organising hen and stag nights.

PROS: You get to sample the nightlife (you may have to do a few test runs).

CONS: You will have to do a lot of legwork, finding suppliers, venues etc.

212. Why not train to be a Masseur/masseuse.

213. Sell business plans.

You could write, create and sell these yourself or you can buy business plans with resell rights. Which you can then resell for a profit.

TOP TIP: You could sell these through local business centres, as well as through mail order.

214. Be a freelance Public Relations Consultant/Officer.
Are you good with the public? If so this is job for you, as your
job is to promote your client, their service, business, book etc.
You need to network and keep contacts with the media and
press, you will get paid to get exposure for your clients
(ideally small businesses). Charge by the hour, and advertise
in local business centres and in local media, press and
magazines.

215. Buy and sell signed football merchandise.
Or how about getting the merchandise signed yourself and
then selling it on. From well known names to overseas
players, there is always someone seeking an autograph,
whether it's a fan or a collector.
TOP TIP: You could sell these items direct to your customers.
For example through online auction websites, or you
could sell them on to shops or stalls.

216. Buy and sell boats, become a boat broker.
Buy or Sell yachts/boats, commercially or privately or link
buyers and sellers of boats to each other for a
fee/commission.
PROS: You get to see some nice boats, and earn a
commission for doing so.
CONS: Same as property, boats or even moorings may not sell
as quick as you had initially thought.

**217. Produce or compose a nightlife guide for your local
Area**.
This could be either internet based or it could be paper based.
Include the best places to dine, dance relax and party. You
could earn money with paper based books by selling to
bookshops and selling them yourself, and you can earn money
with a website selling your guides, by building your traffic and
then getting advertisers to advertise on your website, or in
your books as listings.

218. Hold classes to teach people about car maintenance.
If you know your stuff then when not teach others, for a fee of course. You could offer classes that include what to do if people breakdown for example. You could offer these classes as one to one sessions or provide them at your local community centre/village hall.

219. Why not be a Reiki therapist.

220. Organise weddings, be a wedding organiser.
Everything from the cake to the car needs to be organised. Keep contacts of florists, bakers, entertainers, caterers etc. Take the stress off the bride and groom and their family, and earn money at the same time.
PROS: You can earn some serious money in organising Weddings.
CONS: Bride may keep changing her mind.

221. Create picture books for children.
If you're not really a writer why not create picture books and sell them on locally to schools, playgroups etc. The book only has to be a few pages long and can just tell a story with pictures rather than words.

222. Sell hand painted kitchen and bathroom tiles.
Buy tiles in bulk from manufacturers or wholesalers and hand paint. Resell either directly to customers or onto stores/retail outlets.
TOP TIP: Why not advertise in interior design books, magazines and in your local press and media.

223. Sell old advertising prints.
For example old Coca Cola and Martini prints, (make sure you have the right to resell the prints). Offer a framing service as well = double income.
PROS: Always in demand, and people really like retro prints.
CONS: May initially be hard to source.

224. Make money through Videoconferencing.

225. Create a series of eBooks.
These don't have to be lengthy but could perhaps be based on your knowledge and experience, you could create a series, and sell them with resale rights, people enjoy reading about other peoples lives, trials and tribulations.
TOP TIP: Write about what you know about, and what you enjoy.

226. Sell posters through mail order or through an online shop.
You could sell all types of posters or just specify, for example selling only music posters. Source hard to find posters, old out of print posters, framed posters and signed posters to boost your income.

227. Create, buy and sell information products.
Create and sell information products, learning products and audio products etc for the visually impaired, disabled, or perhaps for people who may have learning disabilities. Advertise and sell through mail order and on the internet.

228. Teach people how to run a business.

If you have experience in business all the more better, but if not this doesn't hold you back, why not take an evening course at your local college, and then teach people what you have learnt and what you know about being in business. Or find out how to set up/start a business and then help people start up their own, charge an hourly rate for example.

PROS: You get to help others have independence and hopefully business start-up success.

CONS: You may feel pressured into making peoples businesses success if you're a passionate business person.

229. Use your website or blog to become a poker affiliate, or set one up.

230. Learn how to spray paint cars.

Why not train and learn to spray cars. You could rent out space at your local garage, advertise in car sales books, and magazines and in your local press. You could specialise or offer a one off service for example that re sprays older models/vehicles.

TOP TIP: Advertise at car shows and at car dealers.

231. Set up and adult phone line/SMS service.

Why not start your own premium rate phone line, selling adult services including services, such as phone chat, adult entertainment etc.

232. Set up a mobile hairdressing/beauty salon.

This could be for men, women or children, or all. You can train to be a hairdresser at your local college, and you could even diversify offering services such as bridal hair, hair extensions. Of course if you are not qualified and you don't wish to be you could always hire the staff you require as and when and you just focus on advertising and marketing your business. You could act as the middleman.

233. Set up your own affiliate programme.

234. Buy and sell stocks and shares.
Or you could join a group which jointly purchases stocks and shares. Although joining a group may reduce your profit it may also reduce the levels of risk, if you want to play it on the safe side .

TOP TIP: Remember never invest more than you can afford to loose and remember that shares are considered a long term investment, typically five years plus. They are not an overnight money maker.

235. Sell a range of novelty products and gadgets.
These could be and are things that people want but will never really use, including gadgets, gizmos, stocking fillers and the latest must haves. Sell these products through mail order, online, on auction websites or perhaps on market stalls.

TOP TIP: Sell through mail order and online to keep your overheads down.

236. Hold acting classes.
You don't need to be trained as really anybody can act. So how about it, if you are confident and assertive then why not hold acting classes for all ages at a venue close to home, advertise at local workplaces, schools, universities, and advertise in your local press/media.

237. Teach people how to cook.
This doesn't have to be teaching someone how to cook a three course meal as some people just want to know the basics, so why not hold cookery lessons in your home or organise a learn to cook session every week at your local community centre/village hall.

TOP TIP: This will appeal to people of all ages, especially single people and students.

238. Write and sell short stories.
How about self publishing and selling your own short stories.
Why not try selling your stories to magazines?
PROS: You get to be creative
CONS: You might not want to share your story with others.

239. Become a freelance reporter.
If you can research information, find information, write about
it, then get it published you could be a freelance reporter, visit
sites such as www.freelanceuk.com and www.nuj.org.uk to
find more information. You could report on news for local
papers and magazines for example, or what about being a
specialist freelance reporter on topics such as sport or
business.

240. Why not be a feng shui consultant.
Devise the layout of houses and rooms that help people
achieve greater levels of satisfaction and productivity in their
lives/lifestyles, business and careers. This is a in demand
service that you can charge an hourly rate for.
TOP TIP: Advertise in your local press and yellow pages, and
perhaps consider giving free consultations.

241. Sell telephone seminars.

**242. Teach people how to use specific computer
Programmes.**
Specify for example, how about teaching people how to use
excel or how to create their own spreadsheets. Why not just
teach people how to make their own greeting cards, or to do
lists. Type up adverts and leaflets and post through
letterboxes what courses/topics you offer, the cost, where and
when etc and away you go. You could teach basic programs
such as excel, or just teach people how to open an email
account (for a fee of course).

243. Become a home business consultant.
Do you have experience in this area, if so then why not teach others how to run their own home business. You could help people print up their own brochures or provide them with local knowledge of the area, target markets etc.
TOP TIP: Advertise your services alongside prices in business centres, libraries, colleges and universities. You don't need experience as you could just act as a consultant and sell your contacts for example, or you could sell research you have collated about your local area, say within a 15 mile radius.

244. Why not start your own cosmetics company.
You could sell home made products, from bath salts to face masks, you could sell through mail order, through home parties or just through word of mouth.
TOP TIP: Make sure you check health rules and regulations with your council first.

245. Create and sell your own DVDs.
DVDs can be made at manufacturers or can be created on your home PC, you could produce and sell DVDs of peoples pictures, or you could sell DVDs that teach people how to do something, or learn something, for example, how to learn to be a better driver DVD.
TOP TIP: See what is missing in the market, for example are there any workout videos for children, is there a demand?

246. Write and sell your own love stories.
These could be fact or fiction, you could self publish them and sell them yourself, or you could send them into magazines, weeklies etc.

247. Open your own takeaway.
What do you enjoy cooking, why not open a small takeaway that is only open nights, what about a sushi takeaway, or fish and chips takeaway? As people are working longer and more hours they are looking for fast alternatives to cooking for themselves.
PROS: Always popular, as people seem to have less time to cook and clean.
CONS: Initial start-up costs may be quite high, when considering premises, staff etc.

248. How about selling life insurance.

249. Open a tanning salon.
If you have extra rooms in your home then you can convert these into private tanning salons, you will need to know and explain all the health hazards/warnings. You could also buy a sun bed and rent it out on a daily or weekly basis.
TOP TIP: You will need to seek permission and advice from your local council, with regards to health and safety rules and regulations.

250. Become a property manager.
Find someone who has one or more properties that you can manage for a set fee. You could ensure rent is being paid on time, you could check nothing has been broken, and you could ensure the overall security of the building/premises. You could offer this service to a number of clients/property owners.

251. Create your own website.

Why not start creating your own website, based on anything from yourself to your interests, to promoting your services and products. You can earn money and monetize your website in many ways, from your website earning through Google ad sense, to becoming an Amazon affiliate. You could even sell advertising space on your website.

TOP TIP: Create a niche website, for example covering one of your interests or hobbies, perhaps something that has a target audience, but not yet a webs presence.

252. Buy and then re-sell liquidation/bankruptcy stock.

Companies and businesses go bust leaving stock to be disposed of. You could buy these products and then sell them on as job lots or wholesale lots to market stall holder/traders, online business owners, locals stores, shops etc. Use the trader, and word of mouth to find suppliers of ex catalogue goods, liquidation stock etc.

PROS: You can choose what stock you want, and cant get it at bargain prices.

CONS: Not all items will be allowed/authorised for sale individually.

253. Become a live in nanny/manny.

Sometimes households require nannies where both parents work, the nanny provides daily childcare and helps with the household work - from taking children to the doctors to picking up dry cleaning. You will be part of the family and are usually employed when both parents are busy professionals.

TOP TIP: To find work you could place an advert in your local paper, or you could register with a nanny service, whereby they find a suitable family for you.

254. Become an au-pair.

Lives with a family in return for doing light housework, this allows you to travel and earn money at the same time.
find work yourself or join and au pair agency.

255. Find data entry work from home.
Don't buy any guides and never pay anybody money to *work from home* but instead enquire in jobcentres, at recruitment agencies and local businesses to see if they have any data entry you can do from home.
PROS: There is always someone who needs help entering data.
CONS: Might initially be difficult to find genuine work.

256. Be a freelance estate agent.
Work for several estate agents, perhaps in different areas, finding and sourcing properties and then charging a sourcing fee. Charge less than estate agencies, contact homeowners with homes for sale, and offer to sell their houses for them.

257. Open a nail bar.
You could take a nail technicians course, manicure/pedicure/nail art course at you local college and away you go. Or if you didn't want to go down this route you could just open a nail salon/bar (based on demand of course) and find suitably trained and experienced technicians to work for you.

258. Open a DVD rental store.
This could be a physical store, or it could be run from home. You could buy second hand DVDs to start up and then rent them out, for example for 1 week, a fortnight etc.
TOP TIP: Find out what regulations you will have to follow when it comes to renting out copyrighted material.

259. How about renting out computer, games console games.
You could build a library of new and second hand computer games which you can rent out for say £2.00 a week. Get people to leave a deposit to ensure they do not steal the product, and run the business from your home to reduce overheads and increase profits.
PROS: Games are sometimes too expensive for people to buy, so you will be providing a useful alternative.
CONS: Rules and regulations may apply as to what you can hire out, this for example may be based on copyright.

260. Become a make up artist.
Why not study/train in make up and beauty at you local college or from home. Once qualified you could work freelance, offer makeovers, consultations, make up/make over's on photo shoots etc. If you didn't want to train to do this then why not be a middle person for an already Qualified make up artist, offer to find them work for a fee/commission.

261. Open an Internet Café.
This is a cafe offering people access to computers for internet surfing. You could charge by the hour. You could also start this within an established café to save on your costs and overheads and to further promote the existing business.
PROS: More people are starting to use internet cafes, to use the internet and to socialise.
CONS: You may have high initial costs/start-up costs.

262. Start a children's play centre.
Indoor or outdoor, it doesn't have to big. Take 10 children plus and charge play sessions at £1.00 (or more) per hour. Or as an alternative you could for example hire out your local village hall say one morning per week, fill it with toys, games etc then charge for playtime.

263. Why not be an Aroma therapist.

264. How about opening a pizza franchise takeaway.
What about starting a popular pizza franchise, or a popular takeaway. See if this type of opportunity is suited to you and your needs and do your market research before you take the plunge.
TOP TIP: Contact pizza franchisers and request more details, regarding start-up costs, locations etc.

265. Open or start a private members club.
Charge a monthly or yearly membership fee. You could have memberships which may cater to certain age groups, or perhaps certain hobbies, for example if you are a music lover why not open a music membership club or something similar.

266. Donate your sperm/eggs.

267. Rent out bicycles/pushbikes.
Why not rent out any type of bicycle from a mountain bike to a tandem. Or organize bike trails/tours in your local area. You could rent bicycles out on a daily or weekly basis
PROS: You get to keep fit and healthy.
CONS: You have to buy the bikes that will be suitable to peoples needs.

268. Open or start a service that rents out wedding gowns, and bridesmaids dresses.
This for example could be run by mail order. You can advertise in the yellow pages as well as in bridal catalogues. Start an off the rack wedding gown/dress hire. Your overheads will be low as you will initially not require premises

269. Produce artwork for bands/artists.
From producing poster artwork, to CD covers. You could advertise in musicians magazines, on musicians forums in your local press, at gigs/halls etc, spread the word.

270. Sell sandwiches, or why not start a sandwich shop or a business.
Deliver sandwiches to local businesses/workplaces, at midmorning and lunchtime. Visit local businesses and get a trial run at first to see if it works out, then if it does pursue this businesses plus others to create a full time sandwich run.

271. How about being a Poll/Elections clerk.

272. Be an In store demonstrator.
Why not be a self employed demonstrator that promotes products for a manufacturer or a store. This could include demonstrating a newly-launched gadget or promoting a new product or range of products.
TOP TIP: If you don't feel confident enough to present a product, why not search for work as a preparatory assistant, whereby you help prepare samples etc.

273. Open or start a self storage unit business.
Or why not advertise your garage as storage space. You could rent out your spare space to people who are in need of a bit extra space. Advertise in you local press/media and classifieds.

274. Offer moving services, man/woman with a van.
Place adverts in your local shops, supermarkets, packaging suppliers/shops, newspapers etc, remember to state what service you are offering and what rates you charge, and how much space you have for example the size of vehicle.
TOP TIP: Make sure your insurance covers carrying materials/products etc.

275. Sell skateboards and skater clothing by mail order.
Why not source individual clothing, from the UK, and even from abroad. What about selling customised clothing and skateboards? Or how about offering a customisation service, and if you can skateboard or know someone that can then why not offer lessons for both the young and old.

276. Sell accessories/parts through mail order/online shop for customising cars.
Not car parts, but more like fashion accessories for cars, From wheel trims to car seat covers.
PROS: People will always want to add a personal touch to their car, from a steering wheel cover to in car DVD player.
CONS: You will have to find out what people really want, what they can't get etc. You will have to do your market research to ensure you don't waste your time and money.

277. Sell children's jewellery.
This could include anything from plastic beaded necklaces and bracelets to Diamond ranges. You could sell direct through an online shop, through mail order, or you could sell through small shops, retailers and boutiques.
TOP TIP: Offer a customisation service, from the design of the jewellery to the colour of the wrapping paper.

278. Clean computers.

279. Organise bus trips.
How about organising trips for the UK, abroad or even both? Start a business organising city tours by bus, or coach excursions to historical sites of interest. What about a double Decker bus for city tours, or an old style single Decker bus for country/further a field trips. Do not buy the buses, simply organise the trips and then hire them as and when required. Advertise your tours in tourist areas, through tourist information centres, as well in your local press and media.

280. What about offering to drive cars.

Drive cars to and from their destination for local car auctioneers, car salesrooms/showrooms, or even for local people/ business owners, families etc. Get in contact with local car dealers and see if this can earn you a bit of extra money.

PROS: You get to drive a nice car.

CONS: You don't get to keep it.

281. Organise days out.

This could be specifically catering to the older Generation or market. Find out what people want, visit retirement homes, organise day trips to canals, cafes, and museums for example. Charge per day or per trip.

TOP TIP: Offer specialist/targeted days out, for example father and tot days out.

282. Organise teamwork events for companies.

Why not speak to local businesses about letting you try out teamwork sessions. This is where you aim to get their business more productive, profitable and successful. You aim to get this through more friendly, motivated and productive staff. Get employees and staff working together and bonding, and you and the company/client will both see results.

TOP TIP: Offer to organise a free team working event for a local business. You want to show them and other business alike what you can do and more importantly what you can offer them.

283. Sell sleeping aids.

Any product that helps people sleep or reduces snoring will always be popular. Advertise your products in your local press and media, in magazines, online and anywhere else you can think of.

284. Create and sell slogan t-shirts.
Why not target individuals alongside businesses. Offer t-shirts to schools, as promotional methods, as freebies, and for people on hen and stag nights for example. Sell through direct mail, online, through other retailers etc.
PROS: T-shirt printing/designing is always popular.
CONS: You will have to build up a name and reputation for offering good quality/affordable t-shirts.

285. How about starting up a local office rental agency.
This is a business/service that is dedicated to the searching, finding and renting out of offices, warehouses and business premises in your local area, say within a 15 mile radius. Offer a one to one service for businesses, you can help them source a business rental that suits all their needs, wants and uses.
TOP TIP: Advertise in your yellow pages, through local business magazines and business centres.

286. How about selling horoscopes.

287. Create and sell gift boxes.
These could be boxes for anything, for example they could be for the day you were born, for example gather items for a person's birth date and year. You could include news stories from across the world, article clippings etc, and sell all in a beautiful presentation/gift box. Market and advertise in your local area, as well as trying to get your products for sale through local retail outlets, boutiques, card and gift shops and anywhere else you can think of.

288. Sell adult DVDs and adult toys.
Why not hold your own parties, sell products online or through mail order. Work independently and sell products you sourced on your own, or be an affiliate sell products for other people and make a commission on each sale.
PROS: Ideal for parties, easy and low cost to set up.
CONS: Deciding how to advertise your service/business.

289. Set up your own donation website.
This is a simple website whereby you write down and tell people what you are trying to achieve and hopefully they will help you in terms of donating a bit of money.

290. Sell holiday/festive decorations.
Granted, this is more of a seasonal business, but it is something you can start at any time of the year. People buy Christmas decorations a lot earlier on every year, so this could be a real money earner.

TOP TIP: If you wanted you could also create a spin-off service that offers to arrange the Christmas decorations/decorate houses and businesses, save people time and money in decorating/designing their houses.

291. Braid hair.
Can you braid or plait, if so why not give this a go, you could work freelance braiding hair, place adverts in your local newspaper, try to get work at children's parties for example.

292. Buy and sell your own mailing lists.
Why not conduct research to make up mail lists based on information about people in your local area perhaps a 10-15 mile radius. You could then sell this information on to locals businesses, especially start up companies.

PROS: Low cost and normally easy to sell.

CONS: Data protection, see what laws apply to you collecting and selling information.

293. Be a home helper/caregiver.
Offer people help on a day to day basis, you could advertise in your local employment agencies, and in local free newspapers/media. Advertise what you do, how much you cost per day, hour, week, and if you can why not offer an overnight service/overnight help.

294. Be a business coach.

You don't have to be a business whiz. You can coach people on how to make their business a success, you don't necessarily need business experience, just a positive mental attitude and hard work ethic. There are always people who want to set up businesses, a lot of them just need motivating.

295. Sell dolls and dolls clothing.

You could try your hand at selling hand made or second hand dolls. You could start a dolls clothes mail order business, whereby you could also offer a finding service: for example finding dresses and dolls from days gone by, and charge a commission for every doll you find for a client.

296. Be a life coach.

Coach people to achieve the best they can in their lives, in family, love and work, again experience is not required only a love and lust for life that can have a positive impact on your clients.

TOP TIP: Cross promote this service alongside a gym/fitness centre to reach even more people/your target audience.

297. Start a relationship advice class.

298. Be an eBay trading assistant.

This is where you sell items for people on the ever popular and ever growing auction site. Visit www.ebay.co.uk to find out more.

299. Sell DVDs by wholesale.

Contact people who are creating their own DVDs and offer to sell their DVDs wholesale, perhaps commission based. Get in touch with DVD production, and manufacturing companies. Network, or just create and sell contacts to people who are interested in getting into this field.

PROS: You are helping others get their work out, and making yourself some extra money.

CONS: You have to be careful what you promote, for example watch out for copyright, fraud, copies etc.

300. Make and sell stencils/stamps.

You could make stencils out of cardboard, laminate them and sell them as multiuse stencils. Sell them yourself, online, on auction websites, through local shops, gift shops, card shops and as wholesale lots.

Chapter 6 Beware of SCAMS!! - How to identify and spot a scam.

Scams are everywhere. Below are a few types of scams that you will no doubt see, when you are putting your own money making ideas into practice. Scams often promise wealth overnight and often take your money upfront and never give you anything in return.

Typical scams such as:

CHAIN LETTERS
ASSEMBLY / WORK AT-HOME
PROCESSING MEDICAL INSURANCE CLAIMS
PYRAMID SCHEMES

TOP TIPS FOR SPOTTING AND AVIOIDING SCAMS

• Before you part with any money, take legal or professional advice because the chances are, once you have sent your money in, you will never see it again.
• There is no experience needed.
• You can work just a few hours a week and still make a bundle of money.
• There are lots of CAPITALISATION'S AND !!!!!! used.
• You read an extremely vague ad. You don't know what the business is about, but it promises you can make loads of money
• You're asked to call a premium rate number for more information.
• Adverts state you can make hundreds and thousands in your first week.
• For a fee, a company will send you a list of businesses that are looking for home workers.
• You are forced to make a decision immediately and are made to feel stupid if you say no to their offer.

MORE TOP TIPS FOR SPOTTING AND AVIOIDING SCAMS

• A friend, relative, acquaintance tells you to come to a meeting at their house. They can't tell you what it's about until you get there.
• And lastly you should think Can I afford to lose the money? Think carefully before sending any money and personal details.

How to Check A Company/Money making opportunity Out

Whether you have those funny feelings about the claims of a company or not, do some background research on them.
Hire a lawyer. This may seem like a waste of money, but in the long run it could save you time and money.
Ask the company if you can talk to any of their happy customers. Please be aware that companies can and will give you false customers to talk to. If these people sound way too happy, be suspicious.

Useful websites to check if your opportunity is a scam include

http://www.fraud.org/internet/intinfo.

www.scambusters.org

http://www.pyramidschemealert.org/html

Chapter 7 – Ways to make money 301 – 400

301. Do voice over's for radio adverts.
Contact radio stations, talent agencies, promoters and anyone else you can think of. Don't pay to join agencies as they are most likely scams. Promote your voice anywhere and everywhere you go.
TOP TIP: Why not place an advert in your local press, local businesses may just get in touch with you.

302. Open a sweet shop or sell sweets on a market stall.
Offer a pick and mix selection, offer sweets from days gone by, toffees, homemade sweets.
PROS: Everyone loves sweets.
CONS: You will have to find out what regulations exist relating to providing and selling food, ether from your home or for example from a market stall.

303. Buy and sell sportswear.
You could specialise if you want to, for example selling old or classic sportswear. Sell online, sell on a market stall through mail order... you get the idea.
TOP TIP: Don't try and sell fakes, there is no point, its illegal and not worth it.

304. Create your own yellow pages.
This could be a directory of specific services for your local area for example. You could start by getting all local business and service providers to advertise for a monthly or yearly fee, and then sell to your local community.
PROS: A good way to build local networks for local businesses and communities.
CONS: Might take a while to build up, earn trust and become profitable.

305. Be a market research interviewer.

306. Train to become a stunt person.
For this special training is required and it's recommended to search the internet for more information. Get all the ins and outs before you commit to anything. Remember it is time consuming and can be very dangerous.

307. Hire out luxury cars.
You could start off with one car, hiring it out for functions such as weddings, proms, birthdays etc. Why not contact businesses that arrange the events mentioned, and drop by with your business card. Advertise at colleges, schools, universities, in the yellow pages, and in your local press. Try also to advertise through word of mouth and try networking with businesses who provide services that are related but not competitive to yours.

308. Start and sell businesses.
If you are confident in this field then why not start a new business and then sell it as a new business, either start trading or don't. People are often searching for ready made businesses and opportunities, which is what you will be providing them with, advertise at business start up centres and through local networking events.

309. How about organising baby showers.
You could arrange everything from location, to gifts to balloons, and charge a fee for all of your time/arranging. Offer an online baby shower service to increase your client list.
TOP TIP: Advertise in mother and baby groups, at parenting classes etc.

310. Start a preschool.
Start a preschool, or how about offering morning children's classes if you don't fancy a preschool. Provide anything from learning activities to fun days.

311. Help people trace their family history.
Help them trace their family and put together a family tree, help people research their ancestry, where they came from, their origin, and perhaps add information concerning the meaning off their family name.
PROS: You help people trace long lost family, and so gain self satisfaction alongside some extra money.
CONS: You might spend a fair bit of time putting together individual peoples families trees.

312. Train/learn to be a Heating and ventilating fitter.

313. Become a dreams analyser.
You could start this by buying books on how to analyse dreams, and then offer your new found knowledge to people (for a fee of course).
TOP TIP: Why not work alongside a fortune teller, this could help increase your workload and business.

314. Start a company or a service that organises pet weddings.
You could arrange everything from pet photography, to the actual ceremony. Advertise in pet shops, local free papers, pet magazines and in local dog salons/pet groomers.

315. Start a language school, or a language tutor business.
Someone always wants to learn a new language or just brush up on the skills they have, why not be the person to teach them, or at least the person to source a teacher and then earn yourself a commission.
TOP TIP: Build a network of teachers, find them suitable work and then earn commission for introduction you make.

316. Hold aqua aerobic classes.
Do this by renting a pool, or section of a pool at your local swimming baths. Advertise the classes at the swimming baths and at local weight loss classes. Offer aqua aerobic classes that are not strenuous on the body but help people get fit and stay in shape.
TOP TIP: Try and rent a pool either in the morning or at night, as this is when you are most likely to get it cheaper, and get your clients.

317. Offer a de-cluttering service for peoples homes, garages and workplaces.
Why not offer to de-clutter their homes and workplaces, but make sure you get there permission to throw items away, charge a daily or hourly rate, whichever one suits you/the job more. Offer your services in the yellow pages, your local paper and in lifestyle magazines.

318. Start a party supply shop.
This could be a shop that supplies everything people need for a party, from the invitations to food and outfits. Supply products targeted at both children and adults. Sell online, through retail outlets and through mail order.
TOP TIP: Get in contact with local events organisers; make sure they use you first for all their party needs.

319. Be a freelance buyer for 1 or more companies.

320. Become a back up singer.
Have you got a good voice, if so then why not provide backing vocals for singers, groups and artists. Advertise in clubs, magazines, bars and pubs. Create business cards which you should always have on hand to give out and expand your contacts/network.

321. Start exercise classes for the older generation.
Why not hold light exercise classes at your local community centre, and charge them per session they attend, hold classes of 20 minutes or so.
PROS: Keeps you fit and healthy.
CONS: You may have to be careful what activities you provide, get advice on what aerobics/exercises you should be Offering to this market.

322. Organise trips/holidays for people who are single.
Not everyone has a partner, and most people like to get away on their own, why not create and sell package holidays for singletons.
TOP TIP: Offer sun, sea and sand holidays, in addition to adventure holidays/trips.

323. Buy and sell comics – buy and sell limited editions.
Why not try to buy and sell foreign comics, limited editions, out of print comics or why not offer a subscription service to your own comic, you could do this online, through mail order, or through auction websites.

324. Sell packaging products by mail order.
You could sell your products to online auctioneers, local small businesses, people moving etc. Source your products direct from the manufacturer or from packaging wholesalers to get cheap products that you can add a decent mark up to.
TOP TIP: Why not offer a printing service alongside this. You could print the companies/businesses name on the packaging products, at an additional cost.

325. Sell your friends and families junk (treasure).
Ask friends and family if they have anything <u>UNWANTED</u> which you could sell for them, and retain some of the profit.

326. Start, produce and sell a local apartment rental list.

327. Sell wider shoes for men and women.
Sell these products online, or through mail order. Most women's and means shoes are too narrow for people. Hold shoe sales for example, to get noticed. You could sell on market stalls and on online auctions.
PROS: Quite a lot of people need wider shoes, as nobody can seem to find the perfect fit.
CONS: May be initially difficult and tiring sourcing the shoes, you may have to look further ashore.

328. Sell tall clothes for men and women.
You could try selling these in the same way as with wider shoes. Specialise in selling this one type of product and you will appeal to more people.

329. Start/Open a cash and carry.
Sell products in bulk, direct from manufacturers or wholesalers, you could sell products from pet food, to toiletries. Open your cash and carry to both the general public and businesses.
PROS: People are always looking for bargains.
CONS: You will have to check what products you want to sell can be resold, check you can sell individual products, and if in doubt contact the company.

330. Join get paid to surf and get paid to read email websites.
This is whereby you get paid to read your email, you may only get a few pence, but hey it's all money, and it soon adds up. Examples of these sites include: www.archerfish.co.uk
TOP TIP: Never pay to join these sites, and check out the useful section as the back of this book, it has links to all the top paying Pay to click, and pay to surf websites.

331. Provide a 24 hour emergency service, from cleaning to rubbish removal.

332. Start a service or business that rents out children's Toys.

Perhaps you could even have a mobile/travelling nursery. Not everyone can afford to keep buying brand new toys, so why not give them the next best thing, why not rent out toys, for example you could rent out a toy for £1 for one week.

TOP TIP: Advertise at your local nurseries, playgroups and day care centres.

333. Sell handbags for men (man bags).

Most men want and even need a handbag but feel too embarrassed to go and find/buy on, make it easy on them, source and sell man bags through mail-order, online, and even on online auctions.

334. Create a company that just sells all of its material in large print.

This is a niche service/business that will earn money if you market it correctly. No bodies eyes are 100%, and so with this you have a good target market. Advertise at libraries, book shops etc.

PROS: You will be providing a useful service. There's always a demand.

CONS: You may need to get printing or even resellers rights, depending on what you want to produce and sell.

335. Help businesses and individuals organise launch Parties.

Promote your service at business start up centres. This service is invaluable for new businesses as most are unsure as to where to start. Gain local knowledge in the area, network, meet people and get connected to make this idea work for you. Organise everything from the venue to informing the press/media.

TOP TIP: If you didn't want to help businesses physically organise a party, why not offer an online service, whereby you offer advice, tips and suppliers from your own home.

336. Why not start a hard to find items service.

337. Create and sell a photo book of your local area.
You could for example collect photographs from the last 100 years and put together in a photo book that shows how an area has changed.

338. Open a bagel/donut shop.
Or perhaps even a kiosk (to save start-up costs). You could offer a wide variety of healthy tasting bagels/donuts from all over the world.
TOP TIP: Make up small tasters to hand out so that people can try before they buy, this will also help build up your business.

339. Make and sell your own cookbook.
This could have recipes for meals that can be cooked in less than 30 minutes for example, it could be a children's cookbook, or a vegetarians cookbook. Or maybe even a recipe book for singletons
PROS: Cookbooks always seem to be in demand.
CONS: Finding enough recipes to make a cookbook.

340. Wardrobe/closet organiser/custom closet services.
Organise peoples wardrobes, try to organise smaller spaces, offer your services to property owners, construction firms and so on.

341. Start a Business men and women's shopping service.

342. Become a relationships counsellor.
You could hold relationship workshops for people who's
relationship or marriage may be feeling the strain. Charge
By the hour. Advertise in local media and at doctors surgeries.
PROS: You will be helping people through difficult times.
CONS: You may feel the pressure yourself if things don't work
out as planned.

343. Become a personal chef/cook.
If you don't feel confident in the kitchen and would like
to give this idea a go, then why not train to be a chef and
once your qualified and trained up go private. Be a live in chef
and you can save and earn at the same time.

344. Become a copywriter.
From magazine adverts to radio commercials books, reports
and articles. They all require copywriters.
TOP TIP: Advertise yourself and your services on freelance
websites, in addition to advertising locally, and in trade
magazines and journals.

345. Write plays.
Write short or long plays and then list them for sale on online
auction sites, in theatre/play magazines, sell on to other play
writers, or, if you want, directly approach
playhouses/theatres. Or you could try and get your play
produced, make money through advertising and ticket sales.

346. Solicit funds for political groups.

347. Offer lawn services.
Not just mowing lawns, but lawn maintenance in general
from grass cutting, to grass treatments, to get peoples lawns
greener. Advertise in you local newspaper/media, through
flyers and word of mouth.

348. Become a scriptwriter.
From radio adverts to children's school plays, they all need scripts writing. Why not browse the internet see what opportunities are currently available, if no opportunities suit/appeal to you, create your own, write your own scripts, sell them or get them produced yourself and make more money.
TOP TIP: Remember never pay any money upfront to anyone, and don't pay anyone to submit your material.

349. Write speeches.
You could do this for local councillors, politicians, business people, virtually anybody you can think of. Place adverts in free newspapers/media and always keep a business card or two handy. Build up your business through contacts, networking and word of mouth.
TOP TIP: You don't just have to write dull and boring speeches why not write after dinner speeches, or best man speeches.

350. Participate in police ID parades.
Why not search the internet or try contacting your local police departments to see if they can advise you further.

351. Be a professional fundraiser.
Get paid to help others and help yourself at the same Time, visit sites such as www.professionalfundraiser.org.uk And www.professionalfundraising.co.uk for further information
PROS: You are helping other people/organisations.
CONS: It may take time to build up a reputation of being a serious and respected fundraiser.

352. Start your own religion.
Maybe a bit wacky it may seem (but is it?) all you need is a few people to catch on to your ideas and beliefs and there you go.

353. Open a vegan restaurant/takeaway.
For animal friendly consumers. You could search the internet for vegan recipes and meals/dishes to get you started. You could provide catering services for parties, functions, local charities and much more.
PROS: You are offering and promoting healthy eating.
CONS: You will have to be selective about where you advertise.

354. Start a Motivational wake-up call service.
Alarms are hard on the ears, and even de-motivating. Instead, set up the phone with your favourite ring, keep it next to the bed, and get a wake-up call. It is an automated service you pay for, and you get a different motivational message each morning - something to really get you going.

355. Chimney sweep/chimney sweeper.
Yes, people still have chimneys, and who knows this could be a niche market for you in your area. There is no doubt this is a messy job but someone has to do it.

356. Be a publicist.
How about being a publicist for or an up and coming writer, author or musician. Everyone needs help in getting recognised so why not help people get known (for a fee of course). You could arrange interviews, get reviews, alert both the press and media.
PROS: You get to meet new and exciting people while earning at the same time.
CONS: You might not get paid daily, for example you may get paid after a campaign has finished.

357. Be a professional complainer/moaner.

How about offering your services to a number of companies, for example to conduct research on how well companies handle and approach customer care, or be a professional complainer whereby the end result is you get items free, which you can then sell on at a profit. Visit sites such as www.howtocomplain.com for more information.

358. Be a roommate finder.

You could for example place adverts for rooms wanted and rooms offered in your area, and then charge each side a placement/organisation fee.

TOP TIP: This would work excellent in and around university areas.

359. Sell phone consultations.

Offer consultations, e.g. offer your own service such as teaching people English over the phone, or sell consultations for other people/businesses and earn a commission.

TOP TIP: Try not to ring when people may be eating there tea, or watching their favourite programme.

360. Get paid for referrals.

For example refer a friend or acquaintance to a company that you work for and when they purchase a product or a service you receive a set fee. Research what products you would like to sell and then get referring people you know.

TOP TIP: Your referrals could be for online companies, local businesses, or maybe even mail order companies.

361. Start a chocolate fountain business.

You could hire out chocolate fountains for events, from weddings to birthday parties, you could run this from home, and advertise with events organisers, as well as in your local yellow pages and local press.

362. Start a modelling agency/school.
Why not hold modelling competitions, book models for events, or if you didn't want to start a modelling school, why not be a scout for a modelling agency, perhaps earning money for finding the talent and then maybe earning money when they model. Could you be a scout for several modelling agencies, hence earning commissions from multiple modelling agencies.

363. Why not become a Stamp Dealer.
You could buy, sell and/or trade postage stamps of the USA or world. Buy in bulk, sell packets, mixtures, sets and singles to beginning or intermediate collectors.

364. Become a food critic.
Try starting off local, writing to your paper about local restaurants, bars, cafes etc, and then build up your reputation by building up your reviews and published articles.
TOP TIP: Why not publish and sell your own guide to local restaurants, cafés and bars.

365. Become an internet searcher/researcher.
Few people can successfully browse or even search the internet for the things they need, so why not find information for them and charge them a fee based on what you find and how long it took you.
PROS: You could work from home.
CONS: You will have to advertise for work, and advertise your services, people wont just come to you.

366. Why not set up/be an Industrial photographer.

367. Be a child psychologist.
Training is required, but once you are qualified you can work freelance, perhaps getting in touch with schools, family GPs.

368. Be a squidooer.
Create lenses on squidoo on anything from cookery to your
favourite book, make money when people buy products from
your lenses and also when people click onto your lens from
Google ad sense. Sign up now at:
http://www.squidoo.com/lensmaster/referral/ljpearce

369. Be a sports agent/scout.
How about developing your local sportspeople and become
their agents, develop their talents, and work alongside sports
clubs and schools to find out new talent (act as a sports scout
for a fee)

**370. Become a salesperson for children's educational
material.**
You can sell these products direct to parents or to schools.
Search the internet for companies looking for salespeople
and agents, selling a wide variety of products from books to
games and toys.

371. Open a tea/coffee mail order shop.
Or perhaps an online tea boutique that sells teas from all
across the world, the same can be done with coffee.
PROS: You are offering a unique service that will attract
people, and maybe even businesses.
CONS: You will have to source the tea.

372. Create and sell party decorations.
How about making and selling your own unique decorations,
for birthdays, Christmas etc... and sell through mail order,
through local high street retailers, on market stalls and fairs.

373. Be a professional finder.

Place adverts that you are a professional finder. Say that you can and will find anything your client wishes (within reason) this could include finding missing people, or just finding a rare comic.

TOP TIP: Confidentiality is a necessity, as people may require items for gifts, presents etc.

374. Why not start a Swimming pool maintenance and Repair service/business.

375. Start a publishing company.

Publish peoples works from your own home, whether they want poetry publishing or children's stories. You could hold competitions to find work and material, alongside asking for scripts and outlines to be sent to your home.

TOP TIP: Don't publish everything that lands on your Doorstep, or else you will never make any money.

376. Start a bathroom/kitchen design company.

Or why not work as a part time sales person for an established business, or perhaps several businesses/companies. Why not offer free design consultations. If you cannot or do not wish to design bathrooms find someone who you can refer to the client, and if the design is successful and an order is placed, take a cut/commission for your involvement.

TOP TIP: Why not offer this alongside a general interior design/ home décor service.

377. Sell camping equipment.

This is an alternative to renting out equipment. Advertise in trade press, consumer magazines, and sell online, through mail order, through a market stall, at fairs and music events.

378. Decorate cakes/cake decorating.

You could buy plain cakes and decorate them for birthdays, weddings, christenings or whatever the occasion. You can train to design and decorate cakes or take the cake to a professional cake decorator and earn a commission for referring work to them.

TOP TIP: Why not sell cake decorations through a small mail order catalogue, to supplement your income.

379. Start an adult website or operate an adult turnkey Website.

380. Start a fat camp.

This is for people who want to lose that extra bit of weight quickly. Why not hold daily, weekly or monthly training programmes. Find a venue, hire professional trainers, advertise then take it from there.

381. Start a nanny/manny finding service.

Find nannies and mannies for families. You could offer a day care service alongside this, that offers a nanny for a day for example, or what about a night nanny service, whereby your provide a nanny for a night. You could advertise at local schools, nurseries and playgroups.

PROS: You can act as a middle man between people and carers.

CONS: You will have to find and keep both mannies and nannies on your books, who may need to be available at short notice.

382. Make/sell/rent out short films.
These could be based on anything from nature and wildlife to how to videos. If you want to produce and sell your own short videos but don't have the experience, why not approach local college students and see if they will help you produce some short films. Pay them per film they create (but remember to retain all copyright etc to the films you make). You could even try selling a variety of short films/series to local colleges and educational centres.
TOP TIP: If you want to rent out short films create a library/short film club, and get people to pay a monthly/yearly membership fee (allows them to see the latest titles etc).

383. Be a lorry driver.
So you like driving? Perfect, why not be an independent driver working nights for example for a couple of local delivery businesses/overnight couriers. Get your HGV license, find work and away you go.

384. Newspaper / Magazine Distributor.
Deliver early morning and evening papers, your a magazine/newspaper distributor so it will be your responsibility to ensure everyone gets their subscription on time.

385. Manage or start a talent agency.
How about getting a variety of artists on your books, then advertise with event planners. Place adverts in the paper advertising your agency.
TOP TIP: Find out what regulations apply to you, for example data protection, alongside what insurance you may require.

386. Start a property rental / sales newspaper for your local area.
You could sell advertising space in your paper. Make money from people placing adverts. Start by covering a 20-25 mile radius, advertise your paper for sale outside/inside newsagents, solicitors etc (anything to do with property).

387. Become a webmaster.
This is the person responsible for maintaining and updating a Web site, includes maintenance, programming, and development of a website/s, you could work contract based to build up your income. Why not see what courses your local college has to offer if you interested in being a webmaster.
PROS: You can be home based.
CONS: Some people seeking a webmaster may require some experience.

388. Run a public house.

389. Make and sell family history videos.
Advertise in your local papers, make videos about people's family history, going back as far as 100 years if possible. If you wanted to you could link this with a family history/tree service.

390. Start a public relations agency.
Its your mission to get your customers and clients in the newspapers, local press media and magazines and you will get yourself a pay cheque.
TOP TIP: Why not work alongside look-alikes agencies, to get up and coming stars.

391. Become a socialite.
Not as hard as it seems, apparently. Basically you are someone who is well known, perhaps a local celerity, you just turn up to events and parties, get seen, maybe promote a company or two while you are there and get paid.

392. Start a newborn announcement service.
This is where people pay you to place listings in the local press etc to announce a new arrival, place your adverts in the local classifieds/newspapers and anywhere else where mother and baby may go.

393. Offer a packing and unpacking service for people who are moving.
Sell you time, your services and your materials, offer to take the stress out of moving day.
TOP TIP: You could link this to a removals or moving service, you might want to offer this yourself, or hand the work over to another company, and get paid for finding them work.

394. Why not Source and sell out of print books.

395. Sell and fit laminate flooring.
Advertise in lifestyle magazines, home décor magazines as well as in your local press. Buy the laminate flooring from wholesalers and manufacturers, offer competitive prices that are below market leaders and you should get some business.
TOP TIP: To gain interest and awareness of your service you could offer a free estimation/pricing.

396. Sell self help books.
These are wide ranging from quitting smoking to improving your memory, people constantly want to learn, so why not feed their minds, and fill your pockets at the same time. In addition to offering new books why not offer second hand books, or perhaps books that are out of print for sale.

397. Start a boat rental/hire service.

398. Get freebies from companies.
Sell these on at markets or at car boots.
TOP TIP: Make sure items you get can be resold, as for example some say they are not for resale.

399. Give blood to medical companies.
If you want to earn a bit of extra money why not give blood, you will be helping others at the same time as helping yourself.
TOP TIP: Make sure you go to a registered company, check with you doctor you are OK to give blood, and overall make sure you are happy with decision to give blood. If you are not then DON'T DO IT.

400. Offer a professional gift wrapping service.
Most people love a nicely wrapped gift, so why not fill this need/target this market. Advertise in local press and media, at flower shops, gift shops, card shops etc. This can be perhaps a seasonal service if you offer such things as Christmas wrapping, or perhaps it could be an all year round service. Start by running it from your home, either gift-wrap the items in your home, while your customer is waiting or offer to sell them the gift wrapping tools and equipment.

Chapter 8 – Motivation – what it is and how to retain it.

Motivation is something that is inside of you, and is something you need to keep everyday if you want to achieve success, make money, or just achieve the best you can out of your life. It is the reason or reasons behind your actions or your behaviour. It is also known as enthusiasm. Motivation is what causes us to take the actions we need to take.

To get motivated you need to write down clearly all the reasons you have inside of you for taking the next step in both money making and personal growth. Write down all of the reasons next to your goals and ambitions, this will create a sense of motivation and importance.

Remember motivation is a key part in becoming successful in any aspect of your life. Working hard, staying focused, spending time with your family and taking regular breaks will all help keep you motivated.

AND REMEMBER

ONLY YOU CAN MOTIVATE YOURSELF!

TOP TIPS TO GET YOU AND KEEP YOU MOTIVATED

• Work and live with passion.

• Be clear about your goals. What you want and why?

• Think positively about every situation you find yourself in.

• Keep all of your visions in front of you, never look back.

• Feel good about yourself, everything you do and everything you have to offer.

• Create and maintain enthusiasm for everything you do.

• Review your hopes, ambitions and dreams, everyday, every week, or as often as you can.

• Always carry with you your goals and aims, and whenever you feel you need motivation look at what you want to achieve and remember that to achieve those things you need to be positive and stay positive.

• Get your family involved, family support is often more important than monetary support.

• Create a motivation space in your office/study/bedroom etc. In this motivation space, keep all of your written goals and aspirations and review regularly.

Chapter 9 – Ways to make money 401 – 500

401. Become a mobile car mechanic.
If you like cars then why not repair peoples cars at their own homes (if its not a big job). People will value this, its more convenient and handy. If you are not a trained mechanic or feel you could do with a bit more hands on experience, why not attend a course, or study from home to become a qualified mechanic.
TOP TIP: Why not also offer car maintenance classes, for people in your local area, to supplement your income.

402. Start an overnight distribution service/delivery.
Start small and focus on servicing your local area/town/city. Ring local companies and businesses, gauge information as to what needs delivering, to who and by when and then see if you can deliver a service that would be more than helpful and useful to them. Competition always exists but provide that extra bit to ensure you get repeat business.
TOP TIP: Are there any local mail order/home based businesses you could work for.

403. How about starting a temporary recruitment agency.
Companies and businesses, especially small start ups are always looking for temporary staff/workers, so here is the perfect opportunity for you. Get temporary workers on your books both skilled and unskilled, inform them they may be required at short notice, then go out and find some work for both them and you.

404. Why not be a Cost Reduction Consultant.
You could do this for either businesses or individuals – tell people and businesses how thy can reduce their costs every week or month, for example by paying bills off early etc, sometimes selling common sense works.

405. Start a launderette, perhaps a coin operated one.

406. Organise breakfast meetings.
Offer to organise and arrange meetings for local businesses, and organisations. Organise the breakfast, the event, the distribution of invitations if necessary, and get paid to organise a short meeting which may take place every month for some organisations.
PROS: Ideal if you enjoy organising events, and socialising.
CONS: Not good if you are not an early morning person.

407. Start a scrap yard/reclaim yard.
Remember there is money to be made in other peoples rubbish. If you don't want to start a physical scrap yard why not just offer to pick up peoples unwanted junk then take it to the scrap yard and to be weighed in, see how much you can get for it.
TOP TIP: Why not offer a free collection of peoples unwanted items.

408. Train to be a network consultant.
Train to be a network consultant who is on call 24/7 for one or more businesses.

409. Start a plant hire/machinery hire business.
This is where you rent out tools and equipment to builders, contractors, or maybe home builders/renovation projects.
PROS: There's always people who require plant hire, and you could start off by offering one or two products for hire.
CONS: Equipment may be pricey to buy new, second hand may be more affordable.

410. How about offering babysitting Classes.

411. Start a mobile fitness bus.
This could for example be an old single deck bus that could be converted into a new spinning studio, it has the advantages of being able to reach more people and has lower overheads.
TOP TIP: This could be ideal for schools, as well as the older generation.

412. Start a gift delivery service.
You could deliver gifts to peoples homes, either working for gift registry/companies, or you could search and then deliver the gift yourself. Search for companies who require a personal touch gift delivery person, for example mail order companies, party planners, event organisers.

413. Start your own affiliate program.
An affiliate program is a way of allowing others to sell or promote your products and services for commission. For example you might wish to make your own music and then use affiliates to sell it on behalf of you. You earn money for each sale they get you.

414. Provide after school care.
This could be in your home for example. Check with your Local council what regulations are applied to caring for children in your home.

415. Sell recipe book collections.
These could be made of recipes you have collected (or could start collecting). You could specialise and sell winter recipes, or party recipes. You could sell through party planning, mail order or through direct mail.
TOP TIP: Why not compile some research into what people look for in a cook book, or what they want to know when they are trying out a new recipe.

416. Become a telemarketer.
Telemarketing is a form of direct marketing where a salesperson uses the telephone to solicit prospective customers to sell products or services. Your purpose is to make a sale, be a freelance telemarketer and work for various companies/businesses to build up your commission. Ring you local jobcentre and small business to see if they have any vacancies, if necessary give local businesses a free trial to prove you can sell sell sell.

417. Start a drop ship business.
This is where the product is directly shipped straight from the manufacturer to the customer without being carried or stocked by retailer. If you decide to start a drop ship service he products you can sell are limitless/endless, from car parts to CDs and books, the choice is yours.
PROS: You are acting as a middle man, and so don't need to store stock.
CONS: You have to have reliable wholesalers or suppliers who almost guarantee the product will get to your customer.

418. Become a hosting reseller.
This is where you sell website hosting packages on behalf of a company. You wont have to store doesn't any hardware. You just generate sales for the mother hosting company, and in return you get a cut of the profit (commission).

419. Why not be a Doula.

420. Get yourself on a reality TV show.
Even if you don't win, it seems you can make money even after the show has finished.
TOP TIP: Being a bit wacky or out of the ordinary never harmed anybody.

421. Start or join an investment club.
This is where individuals group their funds to make joint investments. Each member contributes a certain amount. Money is then usually invested in stocks and shares and monitored by the whole group/club.
TOP TIP: You can earn money by joining an investment club or starting your own and charging a monthly fee.

422. Start a doggie day care.
Why not look after peoples dogs in your own home while they are at work and get paid for it.
PROS: A lot of people don't like leaving there dogs home alone all day while they are at work.
CONS: You must like dogs.

423. Sell your old mobile phones.
Turn your old unwanted mobiles into cash on websites such as www.mopay.co.uk where they will give you money (a cheque) for your old mobile phone/s.

424. Get into property development.
Build, refurbish develop then sell on, don't rent it out just sell it on for a quick turnover and a quick profit. You can be an individual developer or you can join forces (and resources) to form a partnership with another developer.
TOP TIP: Get in contact with you local estate agents, and get on their books, so when property comes up you are the first to know about it.

425. Provide an executive search.
Why not work freelance for companies, find employees that match their requirements, for executive positions, such as an executive assistant. This is kind of like a head-hunter, but you will be specifically seeking people who have the experience and qualifications that your client wants.

426. Why not be a freelance journalist.

427. Be a speech therapist.
Training is required but a speech therapist treats people with communication/ swallowing problems. You could work as freelancer or perhaps for a company/business.
PROS: You are helping people, perhaps be more outgoing and confident.
CONS: Not everyone learns in the same way, and so you may have to devise various learning methods to suit individual clients.

428. Become an internet marketer.
How about being a freelance Internet marketer, provide marketing on the internet for small businesses and individuals. Advertise at start-up centres and in your local press. This is like a normal marketer who sells, advertises and promotes a company and its product range.

429. Join or form a tribute band.
Fancy yourself as a rocker, why not join or form a tribute band recreate your favourite musical group. Advertise for various band members, get the band together, advertise, promote, market, find gigs and away you go.
PROS: Low start up costs, and fun at the same time.
CONS: Deciding who you want to be.

430. Organise gay weddings.
How about being a specialised wedding co-ordinator. Organising everything from location to the honeymoon. You could charge an hourly or a weekly fee. Advertise in lifestyle magazines, your local press, and in the yellow pages.

431. Become a window-dresser.

Go around decorating shops and stores front windows. Provide a decorative exhibition of retail merchandise in store windows. You can work for multiple companies, as well as small, possible independent retail outlets.

TOP TIP: Advertise in your local press, and contact shops and businesses, to create interest and hopefully work.

432. Why not become a pawnbroker.

433. Be an independent/freelance merchandiser.

Merchandisers are responsible for deciding which goods to stock in which shops and how they should be displayed. Predict trends and fashions and decide which products are most likely to appeal to customers. Analyse sales work out targets and plan negotiate prices, order the goods and set delivery dates. You will work alongside window dressers.

TOP TIP: Advertise your services to start up shops/retail outlets, offer you experience and knowledge of your local area.

434. Learn how to play cards.

You could for example learn to play poker and enter in card tournaments. Compete online to get you started, and start off by playing for free. Visit www.pokertips.org for more information on how to get you started making money playing cards.

TOP TIP: **VERY IMPORTANT** (Remember never bet more Than you can afford to loose) and don't always play for money, start off by playing for free, so you can get to grips with the game, see if you like it and can actually play before you kiss your hard earned money goodbye.

435. Train to become a carpenter/joiner.
Carpenters and joiners make and install wooden structures, fixtures and fittings used in a wide variety of fields, including construction, shop fitting, and boat building.
Contact you local college and see what they course they offer that can start you off on the path to becoming a joiner or a Carpenter.

436. Rent out children's bouncy castles for hire.
Granted, this idea requires investment, but this business is relatively easy to run and very popular with children, this could be a seasonal money making idea.
TOP TIP: Contact and keep in contact with events organizers and party planners to get your service well known.

437. Make and sell Detox smoothies.
More and more people are health conscious. Make and sell your own fruit and veggie blended smoothies. Advertise in your local press, as well as at local weight loss classes.
TOP TIP: Check with your local council what regulations apply to you, for example health/hygiene/food preparation).

438. Be a Romantic dinner specialist.

439. Organise boat trips.
Start a business organising boat trips at popular resorts or tourist areas. Buy a used boat for example, or hire one out, hire a crew and advertise where you will go and how much it will cost.
PROS: You get to do and offer something a bit different.
CONS: The cost of buying a boat, and insuring it.

440. Get a paper round.
Look in your local paper for a round which doesn't interfere with your other money making ideas.

441. Supply and fit replacement plastic guttering.
A basic knowledge of how to remove old guttering and replace it with new parts. Visit older homes and advertise your Service in the local press, as well as contacting local property developers.

442. Sell your unwanted CDS.
If you have a few CDs lying around that you no longer want then why not sell them on www.musicmagpie.co.uk you can get anywhere from a few pence to a few pound for each CD, and payment is sent out shortly after in the form of a cheque.

443. Start a dating service for locals over 50.
How about organising speed dating for the local over 50s in your area, and charge them either a monthly subscription or a fee based on how often they attend.
TOP TIP: Advertise in lifestyle magazines, as well as at your local community centres/halls.

444. Be a wine taster.
You can train to be a wine tester and get paid to sample wines from all over the world. Why not search the internet for more information on how you can train to be a wine tester. You could make and sell your own reviews, based on what you think of the wine.
TOP TIP: Remember don't pay to join anything, don't sign up for anything and don't give away your money unless you are completely sure that the opportunity is genuine. If it looks too good to be true it probably is.

445. Why not make and Sell products for diabetics and so on.

446. Make and sell your own herbs.

You could grow herbs in your back garden or in your house and sell at local markets, a very useful book is Start Your Own Herb and Herbal Products Business by <u>Terry Adams</u> and <u>Rob Adams</u>.

TOP TIP: Check with your local council what rules and regulations are in place with regards to your growing and selling your own herbs.

447. Sell pressed flowers.

Why not try your hand at pressing and selling flowers from your own garden, sell them at craft fairs, or sell them on to crafters.

PROS: Low cost to start-up and even to sell your creations.

CONS: Perhaps a seasonal business, it depends on what type of flowers your use.

448. Sell Tupperware by holding Tupperware parties.

Setting up your own home party business is always a popular way to make a bit of extra money, and meet new people. Check out visit www.tupperware.co.uk for more information on selling Tupperware in your area.

449. Stack shelves.

Why not ask at your local supermarket, distribution warehouse or similar, what opportunities and vacancies are there available, consider trying moonlighting, build up just a few hours and you will soon be building up a regular income.

450. Start a nappy delivery service in your local areas.

Buy nappies in bulk from wholesalers and then delivery fresh nappies to houses as and when required. Advertise in your local press, at nurseries mother and baby classes, schools and hospitals.

PROS: You are providing a valuable service.

CONS: You may have to deal with some dirty nappies.

451. How about offering a weed control service.

452. Start a company that specialises in industrial cleaning.
Offer a cleaning service to local industrial units for example; hire qualified/experienced industrial cleaners, to clean every night, or once a week. Find work for several units, or business parks close by to increase your workload and income.
TOP TIP: Why not get in touch with industrial unit managers to see if you can win a contract to clean the majority of the warehouses/industrial units.

453. Start a health food shop.
Why not focus on healthy, natural foods, people are uneasy over products that have been genetically modified or sprayed with pesticides. You could sell organic products on a market stall, through mail order or even online.
TOP TIP: Check with your local council with regards to what rules and regulations are in place, and what needs to be followed.

454. Become a mother or fathers helper.
Why not help parents out by providing an extra hand, for example around the house or on a day out. Advertise your service in the local paper, for example do you have your own transport, remember to include rates, your name and a contact number, or find and train people to become mothers/fathers helpers, and take a commission when they have work, or you arrange work on behalf of them.
PROS: You are helping someone while getting paid.
CONS: It may be time consuming work, as it may involve working out of the 9-5 hours.

455. Start a boutique selling second hand designer clothes.
Why not specify if you want to sell just women's or just men's second hand designer clothes, and then advertise to your chosen market/s. You could buy clothes from market stalls, online auctions or similar, add your mark up and away you go.

456. Why not make wine/be a Winemaker.

457. Make/Sell garden shed and Wendy houses.
You could make, sell or buy them ready made and resell them direct to customers.
TOP TIP: Offer a custom build service, whereby people can design their own Wendy houses or sheds.

458. Sell new houses on developments.
If you have got the gift of the gab then this may just be right up your street, for example you could be a part time/weekend sales person, and earn commission from every sale, ring local housing developers/ new developments and sell yourself (work on a commission base e.g. no sale no fee).

459. Become a children's entertainer.
Fancy being a clown or maybe a magician, you could find work at local markets, or through children's entertainment agencies, or maybe even through part planners/events organisers.
TOP TIP: Advertise and promote this alongside similar services or businesses such as face painting, bouncy castle hire etc.

460. Design, make and sell your own modelling kits.
Design kits that make castles, churches etc. Sell your kits
through art and craft magazines, and distribute to model
shops. Make kits using lollipop sticks, cocktail sticks or similar,
these items can be bought from manufacturers or wholesalers.
PROS: You can be creative, and perhaps make kits to order.
CONS: It may be a time consuming and fiddly job, to
construct model kits using small pieces (time and patience is
required).

461. Why not Start a writers workshop.

462. Design and sell adult games.
You could for example create and sell your own version of
strip Ludo or similar (18+). Advertise in adult magazines/x
rated magazines, and open an online shop if you wish, or you
could hold home parties selling your range of products.

463. Start a floor tiling business/service.
Learn how to plan layouts and calculate the amount of
materials and time it will take when estimating jobs. Build
your knowledge on what kind of tiles are available. Help
customers by advising them on the best tiles/styles. Advertise
your service in the local newspapers and through tile
suppliers, as well as in the yellow pages.
TOP TIP: Offer a design and fit service. Link up with
non competing businesses and services to further promote
your business.

464. Train to become a carpet fitter.
Carpet fitters and floor layers lay floor coverings in homes and
commercial premises such as shops, bars, restaurants and
offices. You could train to be a carpet fitter through say a
hands on apprenticeship. Once qualified target both
individuals and small businesses.
TOP TIP: Offer a free consultation.

465. Start a wheelie bin cleaning round.
Start this service in your local area. Clean peoples bins every other week or once a month for £1.00 plus. Print up leaflets exampling what you do and why and then hand out, or post through letterboxes. Target a 10 - 15 mile radius.

466. Join a reputable/well known paying MLM program.
Multilevel Marketing is selling products by using independent distributors and allowing these distributors to build and manage their own sales force by recruiting, motivating, supplying, and training others to sell products. The distributors' compensation includes their own sales and a percentage of the sales of their sales group.

467. Train to be an astrologist.

468. Supply jewellery making products.
You could do this through mail order or perhaps an online shop. Sell all types of equipment from scissors to beads to ring trees and so on. You could also make custom made jewellery and build up a regular customer base. If you wanted to you could sell your products through direct mail/an online store or at local art and craft fairs.
TOP TIP: Why not compose and sell your own jewellery making kits, which perhaps include step by step guides.

469. Sell Candle-making supplies .
Buy from wholesalers, and manufacturers then sell on to crafters. Compile a catalogue then advertise in hobby magazines, at local arts and crafts fairs.

470. Start a printing service.

Try starting and running this by mail order. Reach a wide range of customers such as start-up businesses, college students, and home based businesses. Start this service with just an inkjet or laser printer, whatever you have in your home at the moment. Print business cards, photos and much more.

TOP TIP: Promote and advertise your service in quirky ways, for example where a t-shirt printed by you, and include your name, telephone number etc.

471. Organise antiques fairs.

Hire a suitable hall and rent out stalls to sellers of antiques. Advertise through local newspapers and posters. Charge both an admission and sellers fee.

PROS: You are earning two sources of income on the day.

CONS: Finding a suitable and accessible location.

472. Why not offer an Indexing service, to authors, publishers and so on.

473. Buy and sell old telephones.

People like old, retro and novelty telephones to brighten up their homes. Sell your products through mail order or an online shop. Source them from second hand shops, online auctions and car boots.

474. Train to be a website designer.

Why not take web design and computer programming classes and then go from there. Advertise your service to start-up companies, this will help build up a positive reputation, which will lead to future work.

475. Grow and sell your own houseplants.
If you have a keen interest in houseplants, and you like growing them in multiple quantities from cuttings taken from mature plants then you can make extra cash by selling them at car boot sales and outdoor markets.
TOP TIP: Why not create an order form, so people can buy there flowers, and so that you can know what you are planting.

476. Why not try your hand at investing in gold or something similar.
Remember don't bet, gamble or invest money you cannot afford to lose.

477. Buy and hire out trailers for cars/motorbikes/vans etc.
This could be anything from horseboxes to car transporters. Buy and rent out second hand trailers. Buy them from auctions, local classifieds, dealers and word of mouth, hire them out the same way.

478. Flower Planting Kits.
How about making and selling your own flower planting kits. Buy pots, soil and seed from your local garden centre, repackage, sell and away you go, your own flower planting kits, which you can sell at car boots and through your local press.

479. Start a driving school.
You may not need to be a qualified instructor (depending on rule and regulations) but this business/service could be hugely profitable. If you didn't fancy being a driving instructor, you could always act as a middleman for the driving instructor, find work for them then take a cut/commission for each new paid student you get them.

480. Produce a workout/keep fit/exercise DVD.

You could sell a workout video for stay at home parents for example, who may not have the time to go regularly to the gym. You might be able to sell and promote this at local health clubs, and healthy eating/weight loss classes.

TOP TIP: Ask a few friends to participate in the exercises, so people can see real life results, and both before and after pictures. Remember not everyone wants to train or work out with a *celebrity*.

481. Organise holidays for golfers, horse riders etc.

482. Start a loft insulation service.

Loft insulation materials are readily available and simple to install. Advertise in your local press, in the yellow pages and through property developers, as well as alongside other trades people.

PROS: You are providing and ever-growing popular and useful service.

CONS: Training may be required.

483. Buy and sell golf equipment.

Buy and sell either brand new or second hand golfing equipment, from clubs to clothing. Advertise at local golf clubs as well as selling through mail order/online store.

484. Buy and sell second hand fridges/freezers, cookers.

Get second hand appliances from house clearances or from scrap yards, and resell making a profit on each one.

TOP TIP: check with your local council as to what regulations apply when reselling used appliances.

485. Start a photocopying service.
You could start this from your home, offer your services to local businesses, students etc. Buy and rent out second hand photocopiers in addition to offering a photocopying service. When renting out photocopying machines offer a pick up and delivery service.

486. Buy and sell second hand books.
Source books from car boots, and house clearances and resell on auction sites or through other sales channels. Maybe you could specialise in selling a certain type or age of book, to help you get even more business. Diversify.
TOP TIP: Visit library sales to pick up some bargains.

487. Why not be a sports referee.

488. Start your own conservatory building business.
Hire out the work to labourers, or become a salesperson for an already established conservatory firm.

489. Buy and sell old newspapers.
Source from auctions, house clearances etc, or what about papers from all over the world, and why not offer a sourcing service. Advertise in local press/media and through word of mouth.

490. Design and produce calendars.
For example these could be based around popular animals, made to order/made to print etc. You could produce calendars for parties, businesses, families, schools and charities.
Advertise in your local press, as well as in the yellow pages.
TOP TIP: Why not offer a free calendar, for example buy 2 get 1 free, to boost your initial business/number of customers.

491. Become a freelance photographer.
Working for anyone from magazines, to individuals, to weddings and family photos. You could specialise in the type of freelance photography you offer, or you could provide a lot of choice by offering a variety of styles, with affordable prices to match.
PROS: You work will be varied, and two days may never be the same.
CONS: You will have to provide evidence/experience to new customers, to show them your capabilities, and build up trust and confidence.

492. Buy and sell second hand CDs, DVDs, computer games etc.
Buy second hand items from online auctions and car boots and then set up from your own home/spare room.
TOP TIP: Make sure you can resale items you have bought.

493. Be a Home based secretary.
This is like a virtual assistant but without a web presence, just a telephone/fax machine if possible, and a PC to type etc.

494. Create and sell dried floral arrangements.
Why not sell your creations and arrangements in craft magazines and possibly online.

495. Buy and sell used/second hand furniture.
Source the furniture from houses clearances, house sales, car boots, the YMCA, charity shops etc.
PROS: There always seems to be a lot of second hand Furniture lying around as a lot of people don't have the time or patience to sell it themselves.
CONS: Storage, and time sourcing quality second hand Furniture.

496. Teach English.
Gain your TEFL qualification and teach people online or in your home how to speak English, charge an hourly rate.

497. Start an evening class teaching basic computer Skills.
From using the internet, to typing a letter. Offer these at you local community halls/centres.
TOP TIP: Why not offer free taster sessions, to get people interested, and to raise awareness.

498. Publish your own newsletter.
Why not create a small niche newsletter that fills a gap in the market catering to your niche. It doesn't have to be professionally produced, but it should be attractive, informative well designed and readable.
TOP TIP: You must find something that you can always write about, for example don't write about the latest fads.

499. Teach people how to make money from property.
Write a book, or produce a DVD on how to make money from property, if you wanted you could even hold a talk either in person or online on how to make money from property. You could gain valuable experience and knowledge by talking to others who have succeeded at making a profit in the property market. Or why not research produce and collate information on local developers (with their permission) and resell to individuals, people are always interested and nosey to see what people/businesses are about.

500. Write books for a how to start.
For example How to start a nursery. How to start working for yourself etc, how to start studying, or how to return books, e.g. how to return successfully to learning.
PROS: Write about what you know, or research a topic, to give people more detailed information.
CONS: Potential start up costs.

Chapter 10 – Money Making Tips

Talk your ideas through with family, friends and loved ones.

Write down any thoughts and ideas you have, its always handy to have a notebook and pen handy.

Don't be afraid to ask for help, remember you never know if you don't ask.

Create a clear mental picture about what you want and why

Never neglect your family, friends and loved ones as they are the basis for you making money.

Do everyday all that you can, be an OPTIMIST.

Remember that anything is possible.

Keep a money making diary. This will provide motivation to keep you going when you don't always feel like carrying on.

Don't get into debt trying out lots of online money making opportunities, most "money making opportunities" have a large fee upfront which you never seem to recoup.

For all money making ideas you use or have write them down, work out their advantages, disadvantages and profit making potential

Differentiate from competitors, always o give 110% to each and every customer.

Stay determined and set yourself personal goals alongside money making goals, for example: I want to earn £1000 profit from money making idea number ... in 3 months.

Chapter 11 – Ways to make money 501 – 600

501. Buy and sell movie memorabilia.
What about buying and selling second hand or brand new memorabilia through mail order or though an online shop. Hollywood oldies, past and present memorabilia is always collectable, and usually easy to resell.

502. Open an American/50s styled restaurant.
an authentic diner or start a 50s takeaway. You could open Provide a new and exciting dining and eating experience. You could even diversify by offering parties, or events within your diner.
PROS: It will be a unique ways to make money.
CONS: Sourcing a diner, or a location for a diner.

503. Sell car guides.
You could advertise your guides for sale in car sales magazines, for example you could sell mini car guides, Austin car guides and so on. You can either make and sell your own guides, or buy and resell (providing you have the resale rights)
TOP TIP: Why not sell through local retailers, online, or perhaps through your own mail order catalogue.

504. Open a smoothie /juice bar.
Why not do this alongside offering detox smoothies. Alternatively you could set up a smoothie/juice cart, ideally outside of universities and colleges!
TOP TIP: Check what health, hygiene and sells regulations apply to you.

505. Why not train/learn to be a taxidermist.

506. Sell everything related to cartoons.
This could and should include well known figurines, cartoon strips, posters, and overall memorabilia. You could sell these products through mail order, through an online shop/boutique as well as at local collector's fairs. Advertise in collector magazines, and could target both the young and old.
PROS: A business that is always going to be in demand.
CONS: Storing all the movie memorabilia, storage needs to be clean dry and smoke free.

507. Design, print and sell your own postcards.
These could have funny designs printed on them, or, you could sell and customise postcards for your customers. You could transfer peoples photographs onto postcards.
TOP TIP: Print these cards up on your home computer as and when sales arise.

508. Start a butler/maid service.
Why not train people to be butlers and maids, and then hire them out for events, functions, business events, or for everyday household chores etc. Advertise and operate with events organisers and similar.

509. Organise makeover days.
Source a hairdresser, a stylist a beautician, photographer and a location, and that's your business. Add your time etc on to the cost of all the professionals, and then find your clients.
TOP TIP: Place adverts in women's beauty/lifestyle magazines, as well as advertising through word of mouth, and perhaps in local hairdressers and beauty salons.

510. Start a company that offers storage solutions for the home and office.
Provide shelving units, desk units, and other products which make the workplace more efficient, advertise in your local press.
TOP TIP: Try offering this alongside an organising business.

511. Sell second hand office furniture.
Source the furniture from businesses that are shutting down.
Only source pieces that can be resold in a short time, place
wanted adverts for office furniture in business magazines and
in your local press/media. Try targeting your products at
start-up companies.
PROS: You are selling useful products, and making a profit at
the same time.
CONS: Sourcing decent furniture that can easily be resold.

512. Start a business that just sells movie soundtracks.
Source your products from car boots, market stalls, auctions
websites, CD and DVD wholesalers and so on. Advertise in
music magazines, collector's magazines, at sales events and
through your local press.

513. Become a wealth manager.

514. Open your own nightclub/bar.
If you like long hours, but enjoy making money, then this is
perfect for you. Or, if you didn't want to go down the route of
opening up on your own, you could simply offer your services,
and charge for them. For example you could arrange launch
parties, staff, suppliers etc.

515. Start a children's gym, gym for children.
Children don't seem to be doing enough exercise, and so this
is your target market. Children's Gyms, concentrate more on
developing children's coordination skills and providing them
with lots of fun physical activity with organized dance, tumble
and exercise sessions. Advertise in your local press as well as
through parenting magazines.
PROS: You are helping children get fit and keep healthy.
CONS: Finding a suitable location that is accessible and
affordable.

516. Become an upholster.

517. Buy and rent out vintage/classic cars.
For anything from weddings to parties and so on. You could
start off with just one car; and this could finance future
purchases, as you get better known.
TOP TIP: Find a car that is suitable for all occasions, a car
that is classy yet affordable for people.

518. Run a franchise.
If you don't fancy starting from scratch then maybe a
franchise would be more suited to you. Why not start
with an established name such as McDonald's, or even
Subway visit www.franchisebusiness.co.uk to see if a
Franchise is right for you, and what they have to offer to help
you make more money.

519. If you are employed ask for a raise.
Ask for a pay based on performance salary, take on extra
responsibility at work, be confident, prepare a list of what you
have done and achieved for the company and go for it.

520. Make and sell homemade pet food and treats.
Why not create dog food catering to dogs with special dietary
requirements, for example older dogs and so on. Advertise at
your local vets as well in the press, and in dog owner
magazines. You could sell your products through mail order,
online and at dog shows.
PROS: You are providing a specialist and niche product.
CONS: You will have to check with vets, and your local
councils what requirements are in place for producing dog
food, perhaps from your own home.

521. Be a forum operator/moderator.
Moderate chat rooms, discussion boards and forums, do this in
your spare time and earn a bit of cash. Search for
opportunities on the internet, but remember don't pay for any
information on opportunities, you don't have to pay to apply
for a job or get more information for one.

522. Start a games salon.
This could include pinball machines, slot machines, bandits and so on. Or if you didn't want to set up a physical location, why not buy the machines (say second-hand) and rent them. Advertise in local press and the yellow pages.
PROS: There will always be someone who wants to play or rent games/machines.
CONS: Deciding which game machines to buy.

523. How about being a Researcher for the media. Why not be a Media researcher.

524. Be a DJ.
Learn at your local college, they might offer free courses in music and music production. Once you have a bit of in house experience start your own mobile DJ business, or start a DJ business and get freelance DJs to work for you.

525. Start your own who Dunnit/murder mystery Business.
Why not use places in your local area, and promote your business all around the country. You could create mystery days, or whole weekends of fun adventure and excitement.
PROS: Its exciting and bound to raise awareness.
CONS: Finding a suitable location.

526. Start a Gothic mail order/online business.
Specialise in selling gothic/fetish wear and accessories. From make up to corsets. Run this from home and if you're creative, make and sell your own creations.

527. Organise home beauty/make up parties.
Or why not example become a Virgin VIE representative, you could offer parties in your own home, or arrange parties in other peoples homes.
TOP TIP: Why not advertise a free party, for example rent out a location, and raise awareness of what you sell.

528. Be a model maker.
Make models of buildings for architects, individuals, housing developers etc.

529. Sell timeshares.
Go along to property exhibitions and see what they have on offer, contact property development/building firms, and find out if they have timeshares, network to find the best opportunity for you, and always leave a business card.

530. Start a home based student recruitment agency.
Specifically for students in your local area – contact local student employers (local businesses that normally take on students) and say what business you are offering. Ask them if you can take on the contract of for example finding seasonal student workers. Get the students and universities on board.

531. Why not start a Kid Parties by the Package.
Sell everything parents need for a Childs party in one box.

532. Open a sports shop.
You could sell products online or through mail order. Sell second hand or new sports wear and accessories.
TOP TIP: Why not offer a customisation service, for example customise a tennis racket, football boots, or goalkeeping gloves.

533. Create and Sell e-books with resale rights.
Give it a try, create sell and market your own e-books, or how about Getting resell and reprint rights to existing tried and tested information products is a quick and easy alternative. Once purchased you can resell them for 100% profit.
Or you can create your own e-book in adobe PDF form and advertise it for sale with or without resale rights.
PROS: Cheap to buy, and relatively easy to sell on.
CONS: How you advertise your e-books.

534. Buy and sell items through internet auctions.
You could buy new or second hand items from car boots, wholesalers, liquidations specialists and then resell your products at a profit. You could sell anything from furniture to Children's wear. Just focus on selling on online auction websites, they are cheaper and have virtually no over heads.

535. Start a mail order/online business selling/supplying equipment and materials for artists and craft workers.
Go on build up a catalogue of products and advertise in arts and crafts magazines. Compile a list of suppliers and get advertising.
TOP TIP: Why not sell how/what to guides alongside offering materials, for example what paintbrushes to use and when.

536. Fit and sell security lights.
Target both individuals and businesses, everyone at some times needs that extra insurance, and what better service to offer. Security lights will tell when people are around, and so will reassure businesses and homeowners.
TOP TIP: Why not sell these products alongside CCTV cameras, or other security products.

537. Why not become a professional bodybuilder.

538. Supply and fit smoke detectors.
Find reliable wholesalers and suppliers. Visit houses and housing estates for work, do door to door leafleting. Advertise and promote in the local press, and away you go.

539. Start a business that just sells items made from wrought iron.
How about selling products that could include beds, gates, or general decorative pieces. You could advertise in home furnishing and lifestyle magazines, as well as perhaps selling through a mail order catalogue.

540. Start a business that helps people buy a property Abroad.
You could act as a UK representative/agent for a foreign property sales company. Take a cut/commission for each sale you arrange.
PROS: You could earn some serious money from commissions.
CONS: You may have to work that little bit harder at times to secure a sale.

541. Start a furniture removals business.
Offer furniture removals for both individuals and businesses, buy a second hand van and away you go. Advertise on notice boards and through word of mouth.
TOP TIP: Produce leaflets and business cards, telling people what you provide and how much your services cost.

542. Specialise in painting and decorating children's bedrooms, nurseries and playrooms.
Target and work for individuals, nurseries, playschools or hospitals. You could decorate rooms with cartoon characters, murals, animals. Or if you didn't feel confident to do it y yourself you could just find the work and then outsource it to a professional.

543. Offer a timesaving service.
Time save for both individuals and small to medium businesses. You could tell them where they could save time, and what they could do to save time. Tell them how they could free up more time.
TOP TIP: Why not offer this service alongside a de cluttering service, as people may want to change other areas in their life, to get more organised.

544. Why not start a school/club for entrepreneurs in your local area.

545. Start a delivery service for shops to customers.
Some shops are not big enough to have their own delivery drivers so why not contact shop managers and boutique owners and ask them direct, if they require delivery people. You could work for multiple local companies and get paid per delivery.

546. Start a special effects company.
You could hire out fog machines, wind machines, costumes, statues, memorabilia etc. You could offer this service to a variety of people including film makers, video producers, plays, shows etc. Advertise in your yellow pages as well as through online sources and word of mouth.
PROS: Special effects items will always be in demand.
CONS: Finding reasonably priced props, costumes etc.

547. Start a secretarial services agency.
This is an agency that has all types of temporary/agency secretaries on its books, it focuses solely on secretaries, from medical secretaries to office secretaries. Be a one stop shop for secretarial services in an around your local area. Advertise through networking, through local press and through word of mouth.

548. Hire out skiing equipment and clothing.
People can't always afford to buy skiing equipment, so what better service to offer. You could rent out the products from your home, and could charge daily or weekly rental rates. You could advertise in skiing magazines, as well as through word of mouth.

549. How about starting a money making group.

550. Write sales literature for businesses.
Or how about writing standard sales literature kits and then
Selling them to new/start-up businesses.
TOP TIP: Find out what phrases sell well, what sales phrases
are commonly used, what works, create a saleable pack,
which can be sold at business centres, or direct to businesses.

**551. Reproduce and sell prints of old buildings and
residences.**
Find out what there is in your local library that you can copy
(that doesn't have copyright of course), or you could compose
books of old prints, or four local area for example, buildings
that used to be there in days gone by that might not be there
now.
TOP TIP: People are always interested in a places, towns,
villages history.

**552. Write books that show people how to improve their
Memory.**
Or for example, write/teach people about learning a new
language. Self improvement books are always popular.
TOP TIP: Why not link this in with some workshops or classes
in your local area, then you can sell your products at the same
time.

553. Sell humorous signs for the workplace.
Why not design and print humorous signs for
businesses, funny poems, quotations and posters
announcing new rules and regulations, are just some of the
ideas that come to mind. Just things that will make people
smile and get them through the day.

554. How about becoming a publicist.

555. Sell personalised books for adults.
Perhaps based on an adult, a family or a couple. Add the adults/characters picture and name to the story and away you go. Advertise your products for sale through mail order, online and in your local press, as well as for sale in local gift shops.

556. Produce a directory of local business specifically catering for the elderly market for example.
Provide an all in one service, whereby someone picks up the book/guide and everything they need is ready for them in that guide.
PROS: You are producing useful information.
CONS: You will have to get businesses to advertise and people to buy your guide.

557. Write articles for magazines.
Decide what your interests are, and what you enjoy writing about, then decide what type of magazine you want to write for. Send in your work to your chosen magazines until they notice you and acknowledge your research and writing.
PROS: You get paid to write about what you enjoy.
CONS: It may not be regular work, depending on what you write and who you write for.

558. Become a self publisher.
Go on, self publish your own work or books, or charge a fee to help other people get published.
TOP TIP: If you choose to write and sell your own material, you could sell it online, through books stores, or maybe even through mail order.

559. Write a book on how to save more money, include useful tips.
Use everyday experiences, your knowledge and your first hand experience. The book could be based on how families can save money, how people at university can save money, how can you save for your retirement etc.

560. Start a savings club.
Where people pay a monthly or even yearly membership fee.

561. Produce a directory of local clubs and associations.
You could for example cover a 15 mile radius of your
town/area/city, and charge businesses who take up the offer
to place adverts in the directory, as well as charging a sales
price to the general public.

562. Write and sell your own quiz books.
Remember to include the answers at the back, make
crossword books and puzzle books for all ages.
TOP TIP: You could sell your books individually to people,
though mail order, online etc, or you could sell them through
wholesale to bookshops, and other sellers.

563. Start a business selling training aids to businesses.
How about selling your own products or being a sales
representative for an established training company.
PROS: You have a wide variety of options as to what you can
sell.
CONS: If you decide to produce and sell your own material you
will have to consider how you will advertise and sell it, and
who you will sell it to.

**564. Why not start a Prom night planner help school and
university leavers get everything and anything sorted for
their big night.**

565. Start a market stall selling sweets and chocolate -
Selling both old and new varieties of popular sweets. Almost
everyone has a sweet tooth and this will prove popular. You
could also visit local business parks at break, lunch etc.

566. Open a shop selling items for £1 or under.
For example, items could include toys, cleaning products, stationery. You could open an online shop selling all types of items for under £1.
PROS: Low cost to start-up.
CONS: You will have to work out exactly what your profit margin will be, as some items may not be worth selling.

567. Start or Open a school for drama and dancing.
This could be a night school or maybe even a weekend school that teaches art and dance to people pf all ages.

568. Start a business selling computer/PC accessories.
You could sell to both the public and to other small retailers. Buy the products in bulk from wholesalers and then resell on to traders/resellers or even to the general public.
TOP TIP: Always make sure items sold in multi packs can be resold individually.

569. Start a seasonal mail order business.
This could for example be an Autumn/winter business, which just sells thermals, waterproof outfits, umbrellas etc.

570. Why not be a Price Checker.
Check out prices for people to get them the best deal.

571. Sell businesses.
How about selling businesses on behalf of others.

572. Start and import/export business.
Find out where and what there is a demand for and fill this demand, this could be socks from Spain, or Ice tea from Italy, create your own niche. If you didn't fancy selling the items you could always import and export for a groups of small businesses, sell onto them adding a mark up of course.

573.Open a computer training centre in your local area.
Hold open classes, teach basic computer classes such as learning to surf the internet, or how to write and read emails, then as your reputation builds up, keep your starter clients by offering more advanced classes.
TOP TIP: Charge by the hour or by the class, as some people may not be able to attend every class.

574. Start a regular newsletter for small business in your local area.
An example could be a newsletter that includes information on local businesses, promotions, seminars, features on local markets and businesses etc... include anything that small - medium businesses will find useful, and worthwhile reading.
TOP TIP: You could sell monthly or annual subscriptions to the newsletter to build up your sales and income.

575. Build and sell computers.
If you have a good overall knowledge of computers then this would be perfect for you, why not buy computers, clean them, update or upgrade them and then resell at a profit. Advertise and offer your services to individuals and small start up companies.

576. Compose and sell a book of poems.
You could either write your own or find poems from other sources, for example place adverts in your local media, such as poems wanted/poetry wanted. Once your book has been compiled sell through specialist websites, mail order catalogues and through word of mouth.
TOP TIP: You could compose a book of overall poetry, or one that is perhaps a little more specific, for example a book of summer or winter poems.

577.Create your own cash back site.
Your sick of making money for someone else, how about
somebody made some money for you for a change, if so then
why not create your own cash back site. You can buy ready
made sites, or build you own, list products and websites to
visit, and research the internet for more information.

578.Produce and sell dog training videos.
Are you good with dogs? If you are it's a bonus, if not why not
be a producer of a dog training video, hire a dog trainer and
then reap the benefits. On the video why not include sections
on such topics as: commands, healthy eating, and how to stop
aggression.

579. Why not make and sell your own games.

580. Produce baby videos/DVDs.
People take lots of photos of their children but what about v
videos, why not put all of their baby images onto a DVD or
video. You could sell your services through nurseries,
playschools, or anything else you can think of to do with
children.
TOP TIP: Be careful about the images you receive, if they
look suspicious, dodgy or just out of the ordinary please
report them to the police, or local agencies.

581.Teach people how to create their own videos/DVDs.
If you know how to create a DVD, or perhaps convert videos
to DVDs then why not teach people, or you could teach people
how to make their own videos, or DVDs perhaps based around
their hobbies or interests.

582. Set up a business that produces photographic Jigsaws.
You could for example produce photographic jigsaws of landscapes, celebrities, animals, scenery etc.
TOP TIP: You could also offer a customisation service, whereby people can get their own photos and images made into a photographic jigsaw

583. Be an etiquette coach.
Are you well mannered, polite, courteous and helpful, of so why not teach other people what you know, and get paid in the process. Teach people how to eat properly walk properly or whatever else they require/request.

584. Buy and rent out your own holiday home.
If you have a holiday home then rent it out, what are you waiting for. If you don't have a holiday home then fear not you can still make money. How about promoting and advertising other peoples holiday homes for rent. Take a fee or commission for every guaranteed sale you make.

585. Open a flower and chocolate gift delivery service.
Run this from home, as it will reduce your initial overheads. Take/receive orders over the internet or even over the phone. Advertise in the local press. Produce business cards and handouts/flyers/information leaflets.
TOP TIP: Advertise in your local press as well as in lifestyle magazines.

586. Start a travelling theatre/pantomime/show.
Produce and put on plays at selected locations around the country, for example at colleges and small theatres. Why not put on/arrange pantomimes around Christmas time. Your will have to find venues/locations, actors, arrange the publicity and sell the tickets, but it could well be worth it in the long run.

587. Find trades people service.
Some people don't like ringing around trades people
and feel like they are being ripped off or lied to at times,
so why not act and be an intermediary for them. Get
them the people they want and charge them a fee for
your time and effort.

588. Start a space saver business/service.
Offer this to both individuals and businesses.

589. Organise arts and crafts fairs.
Start and run a regular arts and crafts fair, organise this in
the same way as a car boot sale. Advertise in craft/crafting
magazines, and charge a sellers fee/pitch hire alongside an
admissions fee.
PROS: It's a creative and fun way of making money.
CONS: Finding a suitable location, and getting your name
known may take a bit longer than you first thought.

590. Buy and sell reproduction furniture.
You could source this from abroad, from car boot sales, and
then could resell it online, on auction websites, or through
mail order, if you have more than one piece of the same
furniture.
TOP TIP: Advertise in the yellow pages and in your local press
that you buy and sell reproduction furniture.

591. Supply and fit car alarms and CD players.
If you have a good knowledge of car electrics, this could be a
good way to make money and work for yourself. Find a
supplier of car alarms and in-car entertainment systems and
advertise your services in the local press. A mobile service
would be the easiest way to start.

592. Sell pre-fabricated homes.
Or how about becoming a sales representative, housing costs are forever rising and so people often look to buying a prefabricated home that they can build to their custom requirements. You could earn money in a number of ways, for example by working for a company selling prefabricated homes, or perhaps by charging a sourcing fee, for example you source the home for the client.
TOP TIP: You could advertise in homebuilder magazines, in your local press as well as in the yellow pages.

593. Start a rubbish removal service.
This could be valuable for people who have extra rubbish – that won't fit into their bins, and when they don't have enough rubbish to fill a skip, charge them for the rubbish removal, and then find someone willing to pay you for your rubbish.

594. Why not start a Cemetery care service.
Provide a monthly/annual maintenance service to care for Gravestones and headstones, charge a monthly or annual fee, this could include keeping the area presentable, cleaning the headstone or perhaps placing flowers.

595. Start your own home parties businesses.

596. Start a roof repair business.
Are you a roofer, or do you fancy being one? If not that doesn't matter, you can still act as a middleman for a roofer and client. Find roofs that need work doing on Them, then find a roofer to do the job, arrange the work and take a cut of any money earned.

597. Start a demolition service/business.
Somebody always wants something removed, but a lot of people don't have the time or patience to remove even things such as old rotting garden shed, or rubble from their back garden so why not do it for them, charging of course. If you didn't want to do the demolitions and removals yourself why not act as a middleman, get the best deal for the client then charge a fee/commission.
PROS: A service that's always required.
CONS: How you will advertise and win work.

598. Buy and sell used sports equipment.
Buy and sell sports equipment from schools, teams, auction websites, car boots and so on, clean up and resell on at markets, car books and online.

599. Start a football academy/school at weekends or evenings for local children/adults.

600. Service and repair gardening equipment.
Anybody with a garden or a lawn is likely to need this service at one time or another. Offer to clean gardening equipment on a monthly or quarterly basis for a set fee, highlight the benefits of good clean equipment and sell sell sell.

Chapter 12 – Money Saving Tips

Saving is important for everyone. It is also useful for building wealth, to save and build, you need to:

Create yourself a budget – identify how much you earn and spend, break it down weekly if possible.

Create a savings and investment plan – decide how much you need to put away and where to invest it, use financial account comparison sites such as www.moneysupermarket.com and visit sites such as www.moneysavingexpert.com to get you started.

Be disciplined – add to your savings regularly, and stop impulse buying and spending

Be patient – saving and building wealth takes time.

Money Saving Tips

• If you have a regular job/income why not apply for an automatic deduction from your pay into a dedicated savings account.
• If you have debts, consider consolidating them.
• Create a budget for clothes and entertainment
• Whenever you feel tempted to make an impulse purchase, think about your goals, then think, Is it necessary? Do I need it? Will it benefit me and my daily life?
• Before making a credit card purchase, make sure you'll be able to pay it off at the end of the month.
• Leave your credit cards at home if you can control your spending.
• Remember: small purchases add up, every penny counts.

More Money Saving Tips

• Start saving coins. After a few months, use the money for household expenses.
• Set monthly saving goals and stick to them
• Install a water meter in your home
• Always use price comparison websites when making any purchase, whether its small or large, for example www.ciao.co.uk
• Get a pay as you go mobile, then you can see how much you are spending, you can get your spending under control.
• Whenever you go shopping create a shopping list, and stick to it
• Try and shop online, its usually cheaper
• Book all of your holidays and trips etc. online and in advance as it will work out cheaper.
• Don't buy it if you wont use it
• Always use items that are reusable rather than throw away items, they are cheaper in the long run and better for the environment.
• Consider own-brand goods – for example when you go food/grocery shopping.
• Learn to say 'no'
• Trade down your car
• Use your library, for books, CDs and DVDs.
• Claim your benefits and tax credit
• Take up a money-saving hobby

Chapter 13 – Ways to make money 601 – 700

601. Make and sell badges and stickers.
You could make these and sell them for or to local clubs, businesses and possibly individuals.
TOP TIP: Why not try advertising in craft magazines.

602. Produce a DVD on how to become a better housewife or househusband.
How about taking real life examples, say from across the Country, and teaching people how and where they can save time when doing everyday chores for example.
PROS: It's a catchy little idea.
CONS: Maybe only suitable if you are married.

603. Buy and sell musical instruments.
There's a wide range of instruments you can deal in. Buying and sell second-hand, import folk instruments from other countries and sell by mail order, online and so on.
TOP TIP: Advertise your stock in selected music magazines and local newspapers.

604. Start a video/DVD production company
You could produce videos, and DVDS for businesses and individuals, from work training videos to fitness videos, and DVDs. Or you could find the work and then outsource it to a DVD production company making a referral fee or commission in the process.

605. Start your own specialised online directory.
Why not provide a one stop resource, where people will go to find information or web addresses for products, for example what about an online directory for apartment rentals, holiday homes, mobility products etc.
PROS: It will be a useful resource.
CONS: Knowing which subject, topic or product to cover.

606. Organise high school reunions.
Why not arrange parties for school leavers, such as 5, 10 and 15 years reunion parties for local schools and universities. Why not use popular reuniting websites to get in touch with classmates?

607. Start a dinner 2 go business.
A dinner to go business could be anything for example it could be where someone brings a ready made meal round to your door at any time of the day, as and when requested, or it could be something like a pre planned meal for 2 dinner to go, whereby it could be a 3 course meal delivered direct to your door. Is there a demand or need for something like this or perhaps something similar in your area.

608. Start teaching an evening class.
Why not hold an evening class in your local college/school/hall etc, teach something you know about, or learn a new skill to teach others, for example how to build/repair a computer.
PROS: Can be a guaranteed income.
CONS: Deciding what to teach, and also considering whether to train in a subject to teach it (if you are not a qualified teacher)

609. Sell embroidery/knitting/sewing kits.
What about selling these products through mail order and craft websites. You could buy the kits through wholesalers/craft sites and then resell them individually. Or Perhaps you could sell knitting and sewing patters through mail-order.

610. Start your own computer classes.
Teaching the basics to 50+ year olds, you could teach people in their own homes, or offer weekly classes.

611. Become a sports instructor.
You could teach classes, adults, children or even retired
people, or perhaps you could train to be a sports coach or a
personal trainer or you could work as a freelance gym
instructor. You can train to be a sports instructor in fields such
as football, running, hockey, tennis etc.
TOP TIP: If you gain experience working in gyms you
could even offer your services to people who are
constructing home gyms.

612. Train to be a music teacher.
If you enjoy music, and have an ear for it, what better way to
make money and have fun at the same time, you could teach
anything from classical music to rock music, you could teach
people how to play instruments from the clarinet to the
drums.

**613. Start a business that runs evening and weekend
courses for DIY enthusiasts.**
You could teach people how they can save money by doing
the odd job around their homes. This is the perfect money
making idea for a DIY enthusiast or hand man/woman.

614. Train to become a dance teacher.
Once qualified in whatever style you choose you could
then teach/hold classes for beginners of all ages for example,
teach anything from hip hop to ballet or salsa. Or if you didn't
fancy training to be a dance teacher, why no just organise
events, or classes such as weekly ballroom dancing classes.

615. Organise watercolour painting classes.
Or maybe even open a small art school, you could organise
classes by visiting local landmarks, places of beauty etc. To
make money from organising painting classes you could fees
for the trip, materials etc.

616. Write and sell greeting card verses.

Write and sell your verses to card companies such as Hallmark, or sell them to individual card makers.

TOP TIP: Verses don't always have to be lengthy and longwinded.

617. Write and produce your own correspondence Courses.

This is easier than you think. Why not write and sell a course based on creating a work/life balance for example. Write and sell your own courses based on everyday life, for example teach people a skill such as DIY, or a qualification such as home furnishing.

TOP TIP: whatever your passion is, write about it, and it will probably be more successful.

618. Write and publish a newsletter.

This could be a paper based newsletter, based on whatever there is a market for in your area. You could even target a niche subject/topic and sell by annual subscription. Compose a monthly research and way you go. Articles and other specialised information could be sent monthly to subscribers. The more valuable the information you supply, the higher the fee you can charge for subscription.

PROS: This is a low start-up cost money making idea, that can be flexible, and one that can be targeted to so many different topics, from farming to card making.

CONS: Deciding what topic to write about.

619. Teach people how to write their own books.
You could teach people through classes through correspondence courses, or you could write your own book. Teach others how to write and produce their own material. Remember don't steal other peoples work (its copyright).
TOP TIP: If you haven't written a book yourself don't worry there is a wealth of information available at your fingertips, from online articles, to library books (just make sure they don't have copyright).

620. Teach people how to build their own computers.
You could hold computer building/PC building classes in evenings or at weekends. You could learn to build a computer at your local college, why not give them a ring and see what courses they offer, you may be able to train in a short time, and then teach others how to build their computers (for a profit of course).

621. Train and learn computer programming, be a computer programmer.
You could learn how to program a computer, using languages such as Java or C++, and then teach others you knowledge, or work as a freelance programmer.
PROS: You will learn something new that will also earn you money.
CONS: You won't learn it overnight.

622. Start a market stall selling computer accessories.
This could include selling upgrades, books, second hand computers, games, webcams, mouse mats, keyboards, printers, software and so on.

623. Design, make and sell novelty photo/picture Frames.

You could make novelty photo frames from a variety of materials, which could include cardboard or wood and you could customise each one to suit your customers/consumers. **TOP TIP**: You could advertise and sell your products anywhere from party planning to mail order.

624. Start a strippogram/kissogram service/agency.

Find models, dancers, males and females, who offer this service. Find work for them, act like an agent, and then take a cut/commission for every booking they get.

625. Frame and sell old prints from books and Magazines.

Search through old magazines whereby no copyright has been granted, for prints/pictures that you can use in your work.

626. Be a speaker.

You could for example be an after dinner speaker, a toast maker or similar. You could even hold speaking events based on and around your knowledge and experience.

627. Be a proof-reader.

Proof read business documents, books, articles, magazines, and websites, just to name a few. Ensure all spelling is correct, and that proper grammar has been used.
TOP TIP: Advertise your services on the internet and perhaps in the yellow pages.

628. Train/learn to be a dreams analyst.

Read up about and learn about what dreams mean, what they symbolise and what they tell us, put together all of your newly found knowledge and wisdom and then dissect and uncover what others dreams mean. Charge a one of fee or by the hour.

629. Collect scrap metal.
You could for example collect copper and steel then sell it to your local scrap yard/reclaim yard, where they will give you money for it. You could also go around local construction sites asking if they have any scrap, and then sell this on.
PROS: There is always money to be made in scrap.
CONS: Finding scrap metal in your local area.

630. Open a petting farm/petting farm.
Why not Re-home rescue animals and open your farm to the public for a fee, you could organise petting days, day trips for schools etc. Earn money through sponsorship of the animals and through admission fees.

631. Start a courier company.
Offer the best delivery at the best prices, be an independent courier, or work for save parcel force. Find work initially within save a 30-50 mile radius.
TOP TIP: See if you can get any magazine deliveries/drop offs while you are doing your deliveries, to double your income.

632. Start your own hotel, perhaps a boutique hotel.
Ideally start small, perhaps catering to a wide variety of people, what about a themed hotel.
TOP TIP: If you didn't want to start a hotel, why not transform a spare bedroom into a chic room which you can rent out.

633. Learn / train to be a marriage counsellor.
Help others get through the tough times, offer advice, help and confidence boosting services for example.
PROS: You are helping to save peoples marriages.
CONS: Will require patience and hard work to build a solid reputation.

634. Start a pest control business/company.
Get rid of unwanted bugs and pests for people, as humanely as possible. If you are interested in this money making idea then why not look at starting a pest control franchise.

635. Open a tapas bar.
Or any type of foreign delicacies bar/restaurant. You could open up a physical location, offer a delivery service, or cater to workplaces.
TOP TIP: Research what people like in and around your surrounding area, how much they are willing to pay etc.

636. Sell your pictures.
Have you got any funny pictures, or perhaps pictures of you with a celebrity, or perhaps pictures of a celebrity doing something they shouldn't be, if so then why not sell them to the media and get some cash at the same time.

637.Become an infopreneur.
Sell information products on the internet, become an affiliate for an already established seller/retailer, sell products such as e-books, CDs.

638. Be a car salesperson.
You could do this either on a part time or weekend basis. Experience is not required and this could be a really good money making opportunity if you have the gift of the gab.

639. Sell your story.
You could sell your personal or family experiences to companies who will pay for your story. You could sell your story to the tabloids, gossip magazines, or weeklies.
TOP TIP: Search the internet to see what is available and what best suits your needs and situation.

640. Sell website templates/layouts and scripts.
How about becoming a reseller, of website templates. Sell
website layouts and scripts, particularly targeting start-up c
Companies. Sell for a few companies to further boost your
earnings.

641. Open a garden centre.
You could either run this from a new physical location, or from
your back garden. You could even start a mail order garden
centre, that sells plotted plants, gardening tools, DVDs etc.
Sell plants, flowers and so on that you have grown
yourself. Or buy products from a wholesaler, add your
mark-up and away you go.

642. Sell customised motorbikes and cars.
You could sell foreign models, models that need repairing and
restoring, or you could offer to source parts in addition to
perhaps buying and selling sell second hand motorbikes/parts.

643. Be a kiosk/cart operator.
A few examples of what you can sell include crepes, coffee,
tea and biscuits. Before commencing with your venture check
with your local council as to what rules and regulations apply,
alongside what licenses you will require.
PROS: Low cost flexible business to start. Can be a real
money maker, if it is situated on retail or business parks.
CONS: Deciding what you are going to sell and where.

644. Be a relocation consultant.
For people moving to your area, or provide advice on
relocating to a new area, for example why not write a guide,
book or DVD, on how to successfully move/integrate into a
new area.

645. Start a baby goods/supplies business.
You could supply nurseries, schools, playschools etc.
Advertise in nursery magazines, as well as in wholesaler pages.
TOP TIP: Contact suppliers, manufacturers and wholesalers
of baby goods to see what prices they can offer, don't always
go with the first one.

646. Sell professional development courses.
You can either create these yourself, write and sell your own
development courses in areas ranging from customer care to
business management or you could be an
an agent for an already established company/learning centre.

647. Open a doll/teddy hospital.
This is where you repair people's collectable and cherished
dolls and teddy's. You could offer a sew, stitch, repair and
mend one stop shop for peoples dolly's and teddies, both old
and new. Start this from your home and advertise in craft
magazines as well as in your local media/press.

648. Copywriting.
Offer your services to both individuals and small start-up
businesses who may need copy producing for adverts,
leaflets or even there website, this is your role, you
create, write and edit the copy.

649. Creating, editing and selling video yearbooks.
Why not create DVD yearbooks for schools/students. Get
together all the material as would be done for a paperback
version and make and sell your own DVDs. Or if you didn't
want to make the DVDs yourself, you could outsource a DVD
production company, and earn just the commission on fining
and getting the yearbooks produced.

650. How about being a surrogate.
How about being s surrogate, get in touch with and agency such as surrogacy UK, for more information on being a surrogate. A surrogate is someone who helps a childless couple have children.

651. Psychological Research.
Have a look in your local papers and on notice boards, alongside searching the internet to find opportunities. Psychological research normally involves exercises focusing on memory exercises or brain scans.

652. Start a School Run.
Why not offer a service for working parents, drop off and pick up there children from school, and other activities, this will provide peace of mind and security to both parent and child, and a bit of extra money in your back pocket. You could find work through a nanny/childminding agency, or from placing adverts in your local press.

653. Invigilating exams.
Firstly get in touch with your local education authority to see what they are looking for in exam invigilators, then if you fit the bill, ask them what work they have available.

654. Debt collecting.
Contact debt collection/recovery agencies to see if they have any vacant position's as well as looking on jobsites, and in jobcentres. Decide on what type of debt collecting you want to pursue, personal debt or business debt? You will earn a commission through debt collecting dependant on how much you have collected, for example you will earn so many pence or pounds of each recovery payment you collect.
PROS: We are in a recession, so you might just have a good workload, and earn more.
CONS: At times you might feel guilty.

655. Open your home to foreign students for cash.

656. Be a dog walker.
Have you got time to spare? If so why not mix exercise with making some more money. Dog walkers are always in demand, especially in cities. Some people do not have the time or perhaps the energy to take their dogs out for regular Walks, so why not do this for them.
TOP TIPS: Why not do this alongside another money making idea such as dog grooming, or dog training.

657. Help school leavers, university leavers and college leavers a job.
Offer a service that helps all the previously mentioned target markets write CVs, prepare for interviews and so on, charge a one of fee.

658. Rent out your garage or driveway to people who perhaps can commute to work from your house.

659. Install and possibly build Playground Equipment.
Build, install (and maintain) playground equipment , from forts to slides, climbing/monkey bars, sandboxes, swings, teeters, circle rides. Design your own or buy ready made plans and patterns. Check on liability insurance.

660. Customise peoples items.
For example some people may want their plain white t-shirt printed on, do one off designs, and who knows where it could lead, maybe to your own clothing line.

661. Writers research.
Help authors, copywriters, webmasters, article writers and so on research there topic. Use the internet, the library and your contacts to find what needs finding out.

662. Start a company that just sells showers.
Specialise in providing a wide range of sizes, styles and types of showers, also provide shower fitting, shower cleaning and maintenance and the selling of power showers.

663. Why not start a baby Items Rental Service.
You can rent out everything needed for a baby's care - stroller, playpen, high chair, etc. When baby's outgrow them you rent to the next people. Advertise, and also send direct mail pieces to all couples with new births (get their names from hospitals and newspapers and mailing lists).
TOP TIP: This could be run alongside and other child/baby money making idea, mentioned in this book.

664. Sell your garden off as allotments, or rent it out.
Do you have a largish garden, if so do you need it, want it or use it, if not why not spilt it up and sell it off as allotments, some people don't have the luxury of having a garden so why not provide this luxury for them, and earn in the process.
If you didn't fancy sectioning off your garden you could always rent it out, for example for parties weddings and much more.

665. Start a spa/health club.
This doesn't have to be large. Why not offer spa treatments from your home. You have lots of choices, for example you could make and sell your own spa remedies/products, as well as offering treatments such as massages, and facials. If you have a spare room in your house, why not turn it into a treatment room.
TOP TIP: Check with your local council, when it comes to sorting out licensing, regulations and laws you may have to abide to.

666. Start your own pod cast.

667.Open a pet shop.
This could be an online/physical shop, or perhaps one that only sells by mail order. Why not specialise in additional services to make you stand out in the crowd, such as dog clothing, or perhaps selling specialist dog food, offer a delivery service with whichever method of selling your choose, as people like choice.
TOP TIP: Provide your services alongside others such as dog walkers, groomers etc, use these links to advertise your service/s

668. Start a Drain Unblocking service.

669. Be a competition organiser for companies.
Work freelance as competition organiser or as an events organiser. Specifically target businesses and help them arrange teambuilding days, in house workplace competitions etc. Offer services that build workplace morale and employee efficiency for example.

670. Why not devise, plan create and then sell a TV game show format.

671. Start an old peoples home/residence.
OK so this isn't really an instant money making idea, or a get rich quick scheme, as that's a scam. With time, effort and patience anything can be successful, if you didn't want to dedicate yourself to a full time residence why not organise trips for older people, days out, club days etc.

672. Buy and sell internet domain names.
As you might already know, domain names are affordable and are easy enough to buy and sell. Find out what names are available go to www.123reg.co.uk then sell on to both individuals and businesses, for a profit of course.
PROS: Low start-up cost, easy to buy, and may have high resale potential.
CONS: You have to find a buyer for your newly acquired domain name.

673. Start a business that prints and distributes leaflets and flyers.
You could target small business owners, and local companies, advertise in local business centres, through flyers, and why not send out free samples to get people interested in your service.
TOP TIP: Offer a wide variety of services from distribution to Design.

674. Create and sell handmade and hand decorated Diaries.
Everyone loves customised pieces, and what better product to personalise than a personal diary. You can customise diaries in the same ways as clothes, by adding sequins beads or whatever the client wishes to have.
TOP TIP: Offer your services to local companies who may be looking for gifts for their employees.

675. Make, sell, advertise and distribute your own perfume.

676. Make and sell your own bread.
You could try baking unusual varieties of home made breads, such as, oat bran, low calorie, ethnic, salt free. Keep a small ad in paper, take orders for loaves fresh from your kitchen and/or deliver fresh to stores.

677. Neighbourhood News.
Write, Compile, publish and distribute a neighbourhood
newspaper (or newsletter) with local news, opinions and
interesting features. Include lots of names; sell space for
opinions, announcements and advertisements. You could
produce and deliver this once a month, for say 50 pence per
copy, charge for advertising and you should soon some profit.

678. Start a business selling home/house accessories.
Why not specialise in perhaps selling bathroom accessories or
living room accessories, from plants to plant pots. Source and
import products from abroad, and supply your products
through a physical shop/mail order or online shop.
TOP TIP: Sell items that may normal be considered out of the
ordinary, to get you noticed and make you stand out from
other businesses.
TOP TIP: Get in touch with designers, decorators, handymen
etc who may all be able to advertise your service alongside
theirs.

679. Why not stuff envelopes for local businesses.

680. How about being a Handyperson.
You could perform handyman services for those who can't or
don't have the time. Advertise clearly what you do, keep your
appointments and guarantee your work (to the extent of your
hourly wages).

**681. Offer an evening class that teaches people how to
make their own jewellery.**
Learn how to make jewellery, and then pass on your
knowledge, experience and ideas to others (for a fee of
course). Hold evening classes, write and sell a book, or sell
jewellery making products onto your students to supplement
your money from teaching. This opportunity has a lot of
potential so if you are creative and have an eye for design this
money making idea should suit you.

682. Sell Magazine Subscriptions.
Sell a variety of magazine subscriptions ads, give credit for
leads and prizes for multiple sales, referrals and so on. Do lots
of telephone canvassing. Have a special every time you call.

683. Busker/Street entertainer.
Get out there and show the world what you have got and try
to earn a few pennies in the process. If you have a special
attention grabbing talent then test it out on the streets, make
Some money and see if you can take it further than just
busking.

684. Start a musical instruments rental business.

685. Build, make, buy and sell Gazebos.
Why not buy, sell and maybe even build gazebos. Sell these
online, through your local classifieds and mail order, also offer
An additional service that constructs gazebos, shed and
similar for people.

**686. Write and sell books on how to keep your children
Entertained**.
Include information with regards to what to do with your
children in the school holidays, and sell them locally

687. How about being a China and Glass Dealer.
Collect, buy, sell and deal in antique china and glass items.
You can buy at online auctions, antique stores, private and
public sales and through your advertisements. Sell on one
cleaned up.

688. Compose, create and sell email marketing lists.

689. Run a dog kennel or cattery.
This is for people who are going away, for a holiday or for business. Why not offer a new service, for example a doggy webcam whereby owners can see there pets. Do you have enough space to take in a few dogs a week, if not fear not, you could always rent some premises nearby if you wanted to pursue this money making idea.
PROS: People have pets and people go on holiday and need someone to look after their pets
CONS: Finding or renting suitable premises.

690. Be a debt Counsellor.
Help people with their debt help them work out budgets, find solutions to their problems, help them cut down and reduce their debts by using perhaps applying and using government initiatives that may provide assistance.

691. Start a time saving service.
Help people to organise their time more efficiently hence their time will be more effective. Offer timesaving advice classes, teach people how to multitask and how to prioritise each of their tasks. Offer your services/lessons to people, businesses or both. Teach people time saving techniques, and charge and hourly or daily rate.
TOP TIP: Advertise your services in a variety of places, from notice boards, to the yellow pages, your advertising will vary dependant on who your target group.

692. Offer a flat and apartment rental preparation service.
Prepare apartments and flats for new tenants, do minor repairs, cover scratches, remove stains, Work with individual owners, rental agencies and real estate companies.

693. Start a house exchange service in your local area.

694. Start a sun bed hire business.
You will need at least three or four sun beds to start with to make it worth while, plus a van to collect and deliver to customers homes. Advertise your service through local newspapers and Yellow Pages.

695. Make and sell flowerboxes
Make and sell flowerboxes for local small businesses and individuals, sell from your own home. Plant and grow the flowers and plants to save on your overheads even more. Buy the flowerboxes from wholesalers.

696. Buy a business, sell a business.
Why not try your hand a buying a failing business for a few pounds, turning it around then re-listing it back for sale, for a profit of course. You could take advice of free seminars, business courses and local business contacts to build up the business so its profitable and ready to sell.

697. Organise Dance Competitions.
Organise competitions in your local/immediate area. Advertise it all across the country, get some judges and make money from admission/ticket sales and entry admissions.

698. Start or hold your own music festival.
This could for example be showcasing all your areas local talent, perhaps unsigned acts and so on. Again make money from entry admissions, ticket sales and advertising.

699. Start a talent show.
Organise and hold say talent show. Showcase and advertise for a multitude of talents, charge people an admission fee to perform in the show, and then also generate profits from ticket sales to advertising.

700. Give drain jetting a go.
If you have a jet washer, or a pressure jet then why
not give this a go. If you don't have one then why not
Rent or buy one, they are cheap to buy, and I'm sure you
will be able to find a million uses for one.
TOP TIP: Advertise your services with door to door leafleting,
word of mouth, press releases, and business cards.

Chapter 14 – Creating a Work/life balance

Balance is key, but, it is hard to achieve when you have to work more and more hours to pay bills, and still find time to spend with your family.
To achieve success with your money making ideas you need to take control in both areas of your life: work and home life. Whether the problem is too much focus on work or too little, when your work life and your home life feel out of balance, stress — and its harmful effects — is the result.

Here are a few ideas to create an effective and efficient work/home life balance.

Keep a diary - Note down everything you do in one week. Include both work-related and non-work-related activities. Decide what's necessary and satisfies you the most. Reduce or delegate the activities that you don't enjoy. Prioritise your activities.

Manage your time - Organise household tasks efficiently. Make sure you have a time and place allocated for your normal daily chores, e.g. An idea is to create a weekly calendar of daily list of to-dos etc. This will avoid panicking and will also stop procrastination.

Fight the guilt - Having a family and a job is OK .

Find some "me time" and nurture yourself - Set aside time each day for an activity that you enjoy, for example walking, running or just listening to music. Unwinding is essential in creating a stable balance.

Set aside at least one night each week as a night off - Discover activities you can do with family/friends. Make time for activities you enjoy will rejuvenate you, and make you feel in control again.

Organise and Protect your day off - Try to schedule some of your routine chores on workdays so that your days off are more relaxing. TIME OFF=TIME OFF. Your body and mind need time off to rejuvenate and re-energise.

ALWAYS Get enough sleep – Working when your sleep deprived is dangerous. Your overall morale, wellbeing and productivity will be low, and this will lead into work being done incorrectly, which will in turn lead to you putting in extra time, just to make up for lost time and lost sleep.

Put these ideas and suggestions into action, it will help you be more successful in money making and in your everyday life. Balance doesn't mean doing everything, you have to examine your priorities and set boundaries. Set time limits, schedules and stick to them. YOU CANNOT DO EVERYTHING, and remember that only you can create your own life balance.

TOP TIME MANAGEMENT TIPS

• Prioritise your time and your activities
• Use time management tools – for example outlook schedule
• Set time for tasks/jobs/priorities – get in the habit of organising how much time is required for certain activities, and it will soon become second nature (hence taking up less time and effort)
• Learn how to delegate – delegation is important that you delegate tasks, as you don't physically have the time to do everything, you only have 24 hours in a day, which after you have deducted sleeping time 8hrs minimum, 2 hours food/rests, only leaves you with 14 hours, so get delegating.
• And finally Create routines, routines for checking schedules, for starting new things etc, one you have established a routine, time management is a lot easier and is more efficient for creating both a life and work balance.
In short manage your time more effectively and you will get more positive results, in terms of making more money.

Time Management – What is it and why it is necessary?

There are only 24 hours in a day. You need to manage most of these hours to be successful in making money, as remember TIME = MONEY.

Your first step to effective time management is to find out *Where you are wasting/losing your time*? For example reading emails, surfing the net. Write down your daily activities everyday and you will soon see how time flies, and how it can soon add up, every second and minute counts.

Your second step is to create personal time management goals, as well as money making goals both personally and for making money.
An example of this could be that you will not take personal calls throughout your working day (unless for emergencies)

Your third step is to analyse and organise your time into a time management plan, yes I know it sounds boring, but if you want to make more money, you need to know what you are doing and why.

You have to change your behaviour over time to achieve the money making and personal goals you've set for yourself. Always track your goals over time to see whether or not you're accomplishing them. Write down activities which are necessary either daily, weekly, or, monthly, and put them into your time management plan.

Your time management plan could be a physical timetable or even a spreadsheet on your computer, which is easiest for you. The target result is that you learn to effectively manage your time, and prioritise each activity.

Chapter 15 – Ways to make money 701 – 800

701. Start a business hiring out marquees and tents.

Most people need tents or marquees at one stage or another, whether its for a wedding, or a party. There will always be a need for tent erecting. You can start this money making idea on very little money as you can buy second hand, good quality used tents/marquees. You could store them in your home and hire them out as and when required.

TOP TIPS: Always have flyers and business cards on hand, that clearly show marquee sizes, prices etc.

Why not collaborate with party/events organisers to drum up more business, alongside your own promotion.

702. Make, buy and sell rocking chairs

Make durable rocking chairs, or buy and sell them as and when required. Offer a wide variety of woods, finishes, sizes and styles to fit each and every customer. Charge extra for carving, special styles or made-to-measure models. Why not offer specials on Mr. & Mrs. Sets, which can for example be targeted towards newlyweds/presents.

703. Start a pet food delivery service.

How about delivering pet food, direct to houses from wholesalers/suppliers. Become a middle man providing pet food to owners homes. This is a valuable service to older/disabled people. Or how about seeing if your local pet shop/s need products delivering to their customers.

704. Start a business renting out DVDs and CDs from Home.

This can be run from home as a mail order club, or from a Get your stock from online auctions, businesses closing down, liquidation items/sales and so on.

705. Why not make, buy and sell dolls house furniture.
You could buy and sell new or second-hand, create one off
pieces and so on. Or, buy inexpensive imported items and
upgrade them. You could sell dolls houses alongside offering
the furniture. Advertise in craft magazines, through word of
mouth and on the internet.

**706. Why not Start a house/building maintenance
service.**

**707. Write a biography about someone living or
Deceased.**
Who is your idol, who do you admire, this could be from a
famous pop star to a historian. Whoever it is and whatever
they have done why not research and write about them. Get
your work published offline, or perhaps self publish it in the
form of an eBook.

**708. Write and sell books on how to improve your
household finances**.
Or how about writing and selling tip cards, from how to cut
spending to how to maximise and increase saving etc. Start
off by advertising and selling in your local area.

709. Turn your hand to Bronzing.
Why not Bronze items such as baby shoes etc. Make
mementos, awards and trophies. You could even design
Unique and one off piece, such as baby's first tooth. Advertise
your products and services in local press/media, on the
internet and through word of mouth.

710. Produce directories of wholesalers and suppliers and resell them.
You could produce, perhaps specialise or just sell general wholesale lists, for example why not produce lists of party suppliers, for example around your local area, and perhaps covering a 10 mile radius. Start-up companies will be a good target market for this opportunity as they often don't have the time, or knowledge of an area to conduct their own primary research.

711. Start a mail order/online business that sells all natural made products.
You could sell products from the sea, beauty products such as necklaces, shower gels, shampoos and anything else you can think of.
PROS: It's a unique, low cost service/business to start up.
CONS: Sourcing the products you want to sell.

712. Offer a Coin searching service.
Offer an individual service, whereby you search for a specific or particular type of coin that you client is after, you could charge a searching fee.

713. Design and print business stationary for local start-up and small businesses.
Print these on your computer, print up samples that you can hand out, or have to hand when networking and posting leaflets through local businesses/companies doors. Also try advertising at local business centres/start-up centres.

714. Learn/train to be a yoga instructor, hold private classes alongside evening classes.
People are working more hours, sleeping less and perhaps eating a bit more, this could be an ideal money making idea. You could offer one to one classes, or in house classes for example to businesses for their employees over the lunch hour.

715. Produce travellers guides.
How about producing travel/travellers guides – its a good excuse to travel, include in depth information on places cultures, customs, historical places of interest as well as popular tourist locations etc. A good alternative to this would be to produce your own travellers/travel eBooks, then sell and distribute online.

716. Write short stories for magazines.
Are you creative, Imaginative? If so, Perfect. You could write stories based on fact or fiction, or if you wanted you could write about true stories that may have happened in your life. If writing to magazines doesn't appeal to you, why not enter your stories into short story competitions(which are held across the country)

717. Design and sell your own painting by numbers kits.
Find out what people enjoy painting and then turn your ideas into painting by numbers kits. Target adults, children or both. Try advertising in your local paper, sell through retailers, through mail order and advertise in craft magazines.

718. Open a training centre in your local area.
How about specifically targeting retirees or similar, or hold one to one classes, or even targeting small start up businesses, the possibilities and opportunities are endless. Find out what retired people want to learn, for example is it computers or maybe a new language. Advertise in your local press and media, as well as through business cards and flyers.
PROS: Helping your local community.
CONS: Might not be an instant, overnight money maker.

719. Buy and sell army supplies/ memorabilia.
Old or new, it is always popular. Why not sell collectables or sell your products online, or maybe even on a market stall.
TOP TIP: Offer a finding/sourcing service to find collectables And memorabilia for collectors. People will pay.

720. Start a key cutting service.
You could start this from your own home, or even from a
market stall, cut keys for individuals and businesses.

**721. How about Photo glazing peoples photos onto
plates.**

722. How about starting a used car parts business.
How about using second-hand car parts can be taken from old
cars. Buy write off cars that are ready for the scrap yards,
take them to bits, and then sell the pieces off separately.
Advertise parts for sale on online auctions, through word of
mouth and so on.

723. Sell telephone answering machine messages.
This is a quirky and fun way to make money. Why not
take/use lines from movies, jokes, poetry so forth. Offer a
customisation service. Market to both individuals and
businesses, advertise and away you go.

724. Start a dog training / dog behaviour school.
This could be an ideal money making idea, with more people
having dog trainers to control problems such as barking,
possessiveness etc, now is the perfect time to be a dog
trainer. Why not start dog behaviour classes, evening or
weekend for example.
TOP TIP: Check with the council what licences, regulations
and insurance you may require to start practicing as a dog
trainer.

725. Search rolls of coins.
Buy rolls of coins from banks and then get searching, search
through the rolls of coins, for coins worth over face value.

726. Sell sports videos and DVDs by mail order and over the internet.
Compile a catalogue of boxing videos, football videos, snooker, cricket, motor-racing and rallying videos. In fact any type of sports video that features famous or exciting events to bring a little nostalgia into peoples lives. Advertise in sports magazines and through your own ecommerce website on the internet.

727. Produce a DVD/CD/correspondence course.
Produce a course which teaches people salesmanship, how to be better salesperson, or perhaps you could teach people the art of negotiation, or perhaps teach people how to have more Confidence.
TOP TIP: You can sell courses door to door, online, through mail order, through sales people and so on.

728. Learn/train to be a painter and decorator.
You could train to be a painter and decorator at evenings or weekends at your local college, why not give them a call? This money making idea has a lot of potential with or without training, as you can do indoor or outdoor painting. You can advertise your services in your local press/media, build up a good reputation for quality and fair pricing, and you should continue to get work.

729. Buy and sell rock, pop, funk etc. music Memorabilia.
This could include records, merchandise signed and unsigned, CD art, band artwork, posters and so on. Also offer a service that sources vintage memorabilia. You could sell your products online, through auctions, or even on a market stall.

730. Start a graffiti removal service.

731. Supply and fit double glazing.
This can be a really profitable business/service. If you didn't fancy doing the work yourself then why not employ fitters to do the hard work. Find suppliers, wholesalers and manufacturers, then find advertise, find work and away you go.

732. Why not start a mail order business selling prints, photographs etc of modes of transport.
This could be for example trains buses and planes, both past and present. Sell to transport fanatics, advertise in collectors magazines, or you could make and sell your own books of transport photography/prints.

733. Start a business that makes wedding DVDs.
People getting married want a DVD to capture their special day. Members of the family want to enjoy the wedding themselves, and so don't want to be stuck behind a camera. Put together DVDs of the wedding plus perhaps clips and images of preparations leading up to the wedding. The DVDs can then be sold on to the couple, family, friends and perhaps people who couldn't attend the wedding.
TOP TIP: Contact wedding organisers, let them know what you're about, your prices and what services you offer.

734. Start a picture framing business.
Offer a framing service for both individuals and businesses, buy the frames from wholesalers, manufacturers, and distributors. Advertise your services in the local press/media, through flyers and away you go.

735. Start a market stall selling cosmetics.
You could buy job lots, wholesale lots from auctions or other traders to get your started. Sell individually adding a suitable mark up. Sell unsold products as job lots on online auction websites.

736. Become an agent for loan company/loan Arrangements.
Loans are as popular as ever, an often loan companies need freelance sales agents, why not be a loans sales person, contact loan arrangement companies and see what they can offer you. You could focus on homeowner loans, student loans or business loans.
TOP TIP: You could freelance for several companies, perhaps working on a no sale no fee basis. To increase your earnings/work load, find or construct your own mailing lists and databases of people who have taken out a loan, or who have considered taking out a loan.

737. Become a freelance sales agent.
Are you a natural salesperson? If so, why not work freelance from your home, kitchen table or selling door to door, you could be a salesperson for mail order companies, or local start-up companies in your area. You could sell a multitude of products from lingerie, to cleaning products.

738. Sell children's and adults toy/battery/electronic cars through mail order.
Why not sell all types of toy cars, or perhaps specialise, sell both old and new, as there are collectors of all ages. Advertise in toy collector magazines as well as in your local press/media, on websites and in your local classified papers.

739. Start a company/service that trains that people in workplaces to be first aid officers.
Train to be a first aid first, then offer your services to both small businesses and individuals.

740. Why not start a mail order/online shop selling work wear and uniforms which can be personally Embroidered.
Buy uniforms/work wear as and when needed from wholesalers, and then do the embroidery yourself or hire and embroider/seamstress. You could target start-up companies who perhaps may have a smaller budget and smaller quantity requirement.
TOP TIP: Search the internet for uniform suppliers and embroidery costs, to get a good idea on what profit you can make per piece, or per order.

741. Supply and replenish water coolers.
Offer this service to small businesses, workplaces, educational institutes and so on. Buy the water cooler from a supplier, sell it to a business or workplace and then replenish the water as and when required (for a fee of course).

742. Perform property inspections for local estate agencies.
This could be for example noting everything about a property ready for its rental.

743. Organise and provide corporate entertainment.
From office parties to leaving parties. You could be a corporate entertainment organiser, who arranges everything from the location to catering. Advertise in your local press, yellow pages and at business centres.

744. Why not sell local tickets/ start a ticket brokerage.
How about selling concert tickets for example. Contact tickets booths and promoters to get tickets before others do, then resell on. Or offer a buying service for individuals where they can exchange tickets they no longer require, in a safe and secure environment.

745. Operate a minicab/minibus hire service.
Get you minicab/private license and away young go. Either work for someone else or start your own service, perhaps specialising in airport transfers.

746. Operate your own turnkey casino website.
This is where you are an affiliate for the casino. For every customer that signs up and participates you earn a commission based on there plays. For example if someone deposits and plays roulette you will make money from referring them and getting them to sign up.

747. Train in acupuncture.
Why not train to be an acupuncturist. Ring or pop into your local college/education centre to see what courses they have on offer. Once you are qualified you can offer your services to both private individuals and businesses.

748. Why not be an Image consultant for businesses.
Find out what colours/styles suit the business. Perhaps work out where it is currently going wrong, are all of its marketing literature the same, if not why? Work out styles for all shapes and sizes, and perhaps incorporate a personal design service, to help rejuvenate or recreate the businesses image.

749.Be an Import Agent for a foreign company.
You could for example find clients for foreign companies that may be relocating to your area, or may be seeking overseas clients/customers.

750. How about Patch working/quilting.
You could try your hand at making and selling your own patch work designs, quilts, pillows or cushions, sell patterns or hold patchwork classes perhaps teaching others how to put their memories into patchwork art.

751. Make/sell hand painted house numbers, names and post Boxes.
Buy basic/standard post boxes and offer a personalisation service, for example painting peoples names and house numbers on the boxes or why not source and sell quirky and different/unique post boxes, either new or second-hand.

752. Be a catalogue distributor.
Why not work for local or well known companies. Get paid per catalogue you deliver, and paid per sale you receive.

753. Help university students organise their gap years.
Talk to your local universities. Match up students with positions, based on experience, knowledge and skills. Charge an arrangement fee for example 1% of the placement costs. Or an alternative could be hat you could compose mailing lists/information on placements, and you could sell the mailing lists to students.

754. How about offering a Baby-Proofing service.
From Stairs, cabinets, electrical cords and outlets-they're all potential baby hazards. New parents, grandparents, and even baby sitters could all benefit from a more child-friendly house. So grab your tools and be prepared to get down on your hands and knees (it helps to view things from a baby's perspective

755. Create Employee manuals.
You could create a standard employee manual, covering topics such as attendance, uniform, training, pay and holidays. Standard employee manuals can then be altered/customise to fit individual clients.
TOP TIP: Target small – medium businesses first as larger companies tend to have a Human Resources section who handle employee manuals.

756. Train/Learn to be an Insurance Advisor.

Why not Advise people on what insurance they will need, why and how much it will cost them. Tell them what companies are available to them, and advise as to what each company offers. You could be a sales representative for one or more loan companies, earning a referral or arrangement fee or you could be an independent advisor focusing on loans, charging a fee based on advising clients etc.

757. Offer a Business-Travel Management service.

Make the skies even friendlier for business travellers, and less costly for business owners. Help book low-price tickets, keep expense records, manage frequent-flier miles, and reap the rewards.

758. Start a mini golf course.

759 Sight Seeing Excursions.

Organise sight-seeing excursions. Pay, point out and provide information to places or sights with a historical or interesting background.

760. Start a Dry-Cleaning Pickup & Delivery service.

Are you clothes-minded? T hen try on the dry-cleaning pickup-and-delivery business for size. Provide pickup and drop-off at a place that's convenient for busy professionals, then follow suit by arranging with a local dry cleaner to do the actual Cleaning.

761. How about offering a Pooper-Scooper Service.

762. Organise honeymoons.
Start offering a unique service. Offer a honeymoon service, whereby you arrange everything from the champagne to the hotel. Act as a honeymoon travel agent.
TOP TIP: Get in touch with wedding organisers and event co-ordinators, as contacts and word of mouth will be crucial in building up your reputation and earnings.

763. Create and sell Pet Toys.
Design, manufacture and sell pet toys. Produce toys that keep pets entertained say for pets that ay be left alone a lot during the day.

764. Why not train to be a Refloxologist.

765. Sell children's books.
With licensed equipment, you can re-publish and sell children's books with their name appearing in print throughout the book. Why not set up a booth/stall in a shopping centre, at a local market, and advertise through nurseries and playgroups, as well as selling online and through mail order.

766. Train to become a plumber.
Trades people are always in demand and if you qualify you may be able to train for your qualification for free at your local college.
PROS: Its good money and its something that always seems to be in demand.
CONS: You're going to be messing with other peoples rubbish/waste.

767. What about being a sports writer.

768. Be a music critic.
Get paid to review songs. Join slice the pie now and start making money, you will get paid based on what star rating you have and how many tracks you have reviewed. Visit www.slicethepie.com now for further information.

769. Become a professional bingo player.
Introduce to your region a service which mounts maps for businesses. Keep a stock of local, national and international maps. Mount these maps in a professional manner to suit the wall space available at offices. Send out leaflets about your services to office managers.

770. Bring out a correspondence course about how to write cookery.
The course might include information about: How to devise recipes, how to present them in written form and what makes a successful cookery book. Advertise in women's magazines.

771. Offer Teaching Typing / typing classes.
Advertise through jobcentres, local press, flyers etc. Offer set lessons and hours, to teach or improve peoples typing, more jobs now require higher typing per minute, and so this could be the perfect time to get typing.

772. Start a Washing-Up Service.
Wash pots, pans, cutlery and plates, for people who may not have a dishwasher, or the time to wash dishes, save people time, and charge a weekly or monthly fee.
TOP TIP: This could be hugely successful around Christmas and new year, when people are having more parties than usual.

773. Start your own 0845 number.

774. Be a rent collector, for example for a rental agency.
Many a landlord finds it expedient not to act as his own rent collector. Call on all the landlords in your town and offer to do this dirty work for him at a small commission.

775. Be an exams preparation tutor.
Help children and adults prepare for their exams. Exam preparation doesn't necessarily mean tutoring or teaching people, you could be an exams tutor who mentally prepares students for their exams.
TOP TIP: Place flyers around schools, colleges and universities, stating contact details, prices, and exactly what you offer.

776. Office/Workplace gym.
Offer lunch time workouts, be a freelance instructor who visits offices as set times, perhaps teaching yoga, or stress relief, whatever you choose to do, advertise your service in the yellow pages, through business cards, and maybe through your own brochure/leaflet. Employers will choose your service as relaxed and energetic employees are more efficient, on time and accurate.

777. Start a car valeting service.

778.The Autograph hut.
Buy, find and sell autographs through exchange magazines, online auctions, as well as in your local press. Offer a finding service, whereby you find an autograph for a customer for a set price.

779. Why not Sell religious products/artefacts by mail order.

780. Start a Picture hire business.
Hire out attractive pieces for an annual fee, or perhaps a one off fee, offer a picture changing service, whereby people can change their pictures every 3 or 4 months, you could also rent out pictures to/for weddings/corporate events.

781. Be a house doctor.
This money making idea provides lots of opportunities, including helping people restore ruins, and helping people sell their houses. If work is required on a house, you could visit the house, see what's required and then find trades people to fix the problems/jobs. You will be acting as a middle man, between tradesmen and the owners, this service will probably prove popular as there are still a lot of people who feel intimidated by trades people.

782. Be an auction assistant.
Some people feel nervous and unsure when it comes to buying and selling at auction, so why not help them through the process of buying selling or both. Charge a one off fee for your services.

783. Get Paid to Post Messages.
There are community forums that offer to pay anyone who joins and posts messages on their forums. The amount you earn will depend on the number of posts you have made. The more messages you post the higher the earning.

784. Why not Make and sell your own hampers.

785. Why not start a Baby Service station.
Turn your car/vehicle into a baby delivery van, providing nappies, formula, baby food etc to parents as and when required, offer a subscription based service, whereby people pay a monthly or annual fee to get the benefits offered by your baby service station, such as delivery of food and nappies, and perhaps hiring of babysitters.

786. Start a Children's Restaurant.
Offer attractive menus, that are healthy and filling, rename adult dishes and plates, so they are more appealing to children, and maybe even offer a delivery service. If you wanted to further diversify why not offer children's parties.

787. Why not be a TV Presenter.

788. Publish a Part-Time Jobs Directory.
Make this a newsstand book, as well as offering it, with small ads, by mail order. List all the possible jobs people can get part-time, especially angling it at college kids on vacation, teachers after school hours, housewives with time on their hands, and moonlighters looking for part-time second jobs.

789. Bake and sell cakes.
Bake and sell all sorts of cakes, sell to local businesses, to local stores and shops you could sell sponge cakes, decorated cakes, fairy cakes, rice crispy cakes and much much more.

790. Start a business that organises sports trips.
For sports fans, why not organise and arrange tours of European football stadiums, or previous Olympic locations and so on.
PROS: You get to organise once in a lifetime trips.
CONS: How you advertise the business/service. People are always weary when it comes to handing over money for tickets and trips.

791. Sell sports/professional sportspersons merchandise.
You could do this by mail order or online. For example You could specify on focus on such things as clothing ranges that have been create by professional sports men and women from tennis to football.

792. Start a business organising Adventure days.
Adventure days could be anything from horse trekking to
bungee jumping. You could organise days for individuals,
schools and businesses. Advertise in your local press and in
your yellow pages.
PROS: You will be providing a wide variety of activities.
CONS: What insurance and cover you may need.

793. Start a tree shaping and hedge trimming business.
People like their gardens and trees to look nice, just the same
as their houses, so why not advertise in lifestyle/gardening
magazines, as well as in your local press, and through flyers.
Business cards and word of mouth will also prove essential in
building up your name and income.
TOP TIP: Why not offer a free consultation.

794. Write press releases for new start up businesses.
Some businesses and individuals cannot write a press
release, so help them out, write one for them, you will
find lots of information on creating, writing a
structuring a press release so get going. Earn money for
writing a press release for a new company and so on.

**795. Why not be a Desktop publisher, or offer desktop
publishing services.**

796. Produce, offer, buy and sell Intelligence Tests.
People are always interested in learning about themselves,
sell intelligence tests through your local press and online, help
people find out abut their work, life, problems and abilities.
Compile tests by using and conducting research into what
people want to know about themselves.

797. Start a Linen Supply service.
Why not provide homes with fresh towels and sheets, for example once a week, start a delivery route say 15 mile radius and charge a monthly linen fee.
TOP TIP: Offer your services to local businesses such as restaurants and hotels.

798. Pre-Christmas Parties.
You could sell party items through mail order and party plan, you could sell everything people need at Christmas, from hampers to stocking fillers, and from decorations to food and drink.

799. Why not start a locating businesses.
Help people who were adopted find their birth parents and so on.

800. Write and sell tips booklets.
You could write these based on your experience and knowledge. It could be based on keeping children entertained, or how to attract the opposite, whatever you feel you have to write about.

Chapter 16 – How to make your money work for you

There are lots of ways you can make your money work for you, for example putting your money away into a savings bond, investing your money in premium bonds, or what about stocks and shares?

Compounding interest

Compounding means that you earn interest on your interest. When you keep the interest your money earns in savings account, bond etc, it will earn interest, too.
Remember that interest rates make a difference.

Ways to make your money work for you include:

Save up to £3600 in a cash ISA.
Save more in a cash/stock/share ISA.
Pay regularly into a premium savers account, most banks offer them, and the yearly interest is normally higher than standard accounts.
Put money into premium bonds, lose interest but hope it makes you more money in the long run.
Invest in the stock market.

Go forth and multiply To make more money, you have to have some in the first place. You can maximise what you have, no matter how little.

TIPS ON HOW TO MAKE YOUR MONEY WORK FOR YOU
Find savings accounts with the highest interest rates, use money comparison websites. Make sure you can account for money spent and saved, keep a spending/saving diary.

Chapter 17 - Ways to make money 801 – 900

801. Provide and sell Magazine Back Issues.
Or why not be Magazine Back Issues trader or locater. If a customer requests for a specific issue which you don't have, you'll need to know where you can get a copy. If there are too many magazines to keep stock, you might want to consider specializing. Automotive magazines would be a good example. People are often looking for back issues of good automotive magazines for the vehicle reviews and the technical section.

802. Start your own gossip newsletter or paper.

803. Start a Day labour agency.
Create databases of both people who are searching day labour and companies that require day labourers. Charge a fee for arranging a placement.

804. Why not start a Hospital grooming service.
Offer your service to people who like to take car off themselves and their image, or perhaps those who have little family to help them out. Offer services such as hairstyling, nail and feet care. Dependant on hour long care is required, you could charge an hourly or weekly fee.

805. Run a Floor Scraping/Polishing Service.
You buy or (at first) rent, a heavy-duty machine, and do the cleaning and waxing of fine, hardwood floors. If the floors are in very bad condition, machine sand them and them completely refinish them with modern super-durable polyurethane finishes.

806. Make money with awning and windows.
Design and install permanent and fold-up fabric and or metal awnings for storefronts, patios, house windows, trailers and mobile homes. Offer a selection of materials, colours and prices. Advertise prices and benefits.

807. Why not get into Lapidary/Gem Making.
You could start and Operate a rock shop in your garage. Cut, polish facet, shape and mount gems in commercial and amateur findings. Sell mounted, un mounted gems and jewellery. Tumble imperfections and left-over's to sell Separately.

808. How about selling Imported food delicacies.
Obtain items that cannot easily be bought, people like to try new things, so why not offer tasting sessions, to build up your reputation and service.

809. Start offering Childbirth Classes.
Teach new parents all they need to know, what to do and how.

810. Why not offer Business Skills Class.
Teach others how to run a business, how to make and save money.

811. Teach people how to improve their confidence and self esteem.
Maybe you could produce and write small books/booklets based on these and similar topics, hold confidence boosting classes, one to one sessions, and what about possible offering confidence building workshops to generate more income?.
TOP TIP: Target both individuals and companies.

812. Become a private detective.
You can start this for virtually next to nothing, and you could advertise in the yellow pages, magazines and any other relevant press and media/ directories. You could also work for an agency as a freelance and charge by the hour.
TOP TIP: Find out what data protection laws apply to finding out more information on people/businesses.

813. Become an online tutor.
Place adverts on internet boards that you are an online tutor, for example you could be an online English tutor who teaches English to foreign people/students/businessmen etc, use your webcam or for example applications such as Skype to communicate.
PROS: Low cost, no real overheads.
CONS: Hours may vary as you need to be able to accommodate your students.

814. Become a personal stylist.
From hair, to clothes and nails. Learn what styles and outfits suite certain body types and then sell your knowledge and experience.
TOP TIP: Why not offer this alongside creating and selling your own experience/makeover days, or perhaps offering a personal shopper service.

815. Start a car rental company.
Every one needs a car at some point. Why not help people and help yourself at the same time by renting out cars, you could advertise in your local press and rent out new or used cars for a weekly or monthly fee. Or how about teaming up with/working for a large hire company as an affiliate, generating sales for them then taking a cut/commission.

816. Buy and sell Cheap power tools.

817. Sell larger shoes for both men and women.
More people have larger feet, and the conventional shops
don't cater for people with bigger feet, so why not fill this
need, set up a retail/wholesale business, buy surplus stock,
sell products on market stalls etc, just anywhere and
everywhere you can think of that would reach your target
market.

818. Set up a weekly speed dating session/business.
Hold these at your local community centre/village hall, and
charge say £2.00 per person, per event attended.
PROS: There is always a demand for dating sessions within
local communities.
CONS: May take a while to build up a dating database, as
people may be a bit nervous to join your club at first.

**819. Get on who wants to be a Millionaire, or a similar
quiz show/game show.**

**820. Why not buy material and make soft furnishings to
sell**.
You could also take the material to get made up into things
such as curtains, cushions, bedcovers etc which you can then
sell on individually. Offer a design service to generate more
business and get out there and advertise. People love
handmade and hand created furnishings.
TOP TIP: Get in touch with interior designers. Tell them
about your service.

821. Offer/start a Computer Consulting service.

822. Offer a walking tour guide service.
Research your local area, its history, popular tourist spots etc.
Plan a historical tour around places of interest within
reasonable walking distance. Inform the local tourist
information centre. Leave leaflets for tourists to let them
know where to find you.
TOP TIP: Three or four tours a day will help you make
money, as well as diversifying an offering your services to
college/school/university groups, foreign exchange visitors.

823. Start a party plan business.
Good organisational skills are required, as well as the ability
to sell and network. Read up on companies that offer party
plan, and see what they do and don't offer, and then decide
from your research what is needed, then GO FOR IT. Offer
products not widely available in shops, or if you choose too,
why not be a party plan host for a more well known
company/brand, to get you some extra cash.
PROS: Low start-up costs, and you can learn as your going
along.
CONS: Knowing what products you are going to sell and why,
do they fulfil a need, satisfy a want.

**824. Give music lessons or organise music lessons be an
intermediary.**

825. Buy and sell second hand keep-fit equipment.
Some people don't feel comfortable attending a gym, and some
people cant afford new equipment, they don't want to pay out
large amounts of money and would probably prefer to workout
in the privacy of their own homes, so accommodate them. As
well as offering this service, you could try buying and selling
second hand gym equipment, see if this generates some extra
income.
TOP TIP: Buy the equipment from gyms that are shutting
down or in the process of refurbishment.

826. Why not start a Reminder service, for both individuals and Businesses.
Send an email, an SMS message, or phone them, to remind them to do something.

827. What about Creating, buy and selling Study posters
For example Common Spanish verbs for Spanish students
Common math equations for calculus students.
Sell to schools, colleges, test preparation centres and companies.

828. Send in your video to you've been framed, and get £250 for it.

829. Why not design and sell custom cookbooks.
Decorate (personalize the cover) and custom print peoples recipe collections - into their own family Cookbook and so on.

830. Start a Companion Service.
Accompany lonely, ailing or elderly people alone temporarily, on shopping trips, to and from the doctor, on short tours or when travelling longer distances.

831. Sex aids are a good mail order seller.
As you might guess, not everyone feels comfortable going into a shop to purchase these type of products. A mail order business set up to provide an exciting range of naughty toys and sexy underwear can hardly fail, providing a sensible approach to business is maintained. Seek out suppliers through suitable trade directories and magazines such as `The Trader.

832. Why not start a Sunday morning delivery service.
You could for example deliver breakfast and paper to homes. Offer various packages, such as a Sunday paper, and breakfast for only £5.95.

833. Train to be a pet photographer/ Get into Pet photography.

834. Make and sell Baby food.
Make and sell homemade baby food. Specialize in mixing, processing, packaging and selling homemade natural baby foods. Licensing and insurance required, dedicated work area strongly recommended.
TOP TIP: Contact your local council, see what rules and regulations are in place, what needs to be applied and followed.

835. Why not start an Appointment confirming service Appointments.
You call and confirm their clients appointments.

836. Produce DVD Brochures
Make DVD brochures for small start up companies and so on. Advertise and market at local start up events, centres, through press release, door to door marketing and word of mouth.

837. Offer a Workplace design service.
You could be a creator of the workplace of the future Environments, office spaces and so on.

838. Why not distribute new and upcoming artists material.
For example CDs and books, and charge them a commission of £1.00 for each product you sell

839. How about starting an appliance repair service

840. Why not start an Artificial Plants business.
Make your specialty artificial flowers and plants. Sell a selection of arrangements, baskets and special occasion creations; take custom orders.

841. How about setting up an internet store without having to stock your own products.
You could create an eCommerce online store, that is readily stocked with quality merchandise and equipped with credit card processing, order fulfilment and customer service.
TOP TIP: You could try initially catering to one market, don't try and diversify and sell everything at once, it will not work.

842. Why not start your own business selling health foods and supplements.
These products are light and easy to post, and you could sell them through mail order, catalogues, home parties and direct mail. Advertise in health and leisure magazines, if you want to go it alone. If not, why not work as an agent for one of the Leading companies.
PROS: More people will want to get fit and healthy, and you will be helping them.
CONS: Check out what products you are selling, are they recognised, healthy, legal and suitable for the market etc.

843. Have a go at selling business manuals and self improvement guides by post, and by email.
Planning and organisational skills are a must but you can write and self-publish your own material and see if it sells. Or you can buy material that has resell rights and sell this. You could even try selling it over the internet and through local business networks and chambers of commerce.
TOP TIP: Research your local business market to find out what they would like to know more about, for example is it their local area, how they can advertise in that area, how they can reach their target markets etc.

844. How about buying and rent out decorating tools and equipment to DIY decorators and small businesses.

845. Start a Concierge.
If you have a lot of energy, a love for the mundane, and the ability to Juggle multiple tasks, consider providing a personal concierge to busy business people or parents.

846. Provide Home Inventories.
For when people require home/contents insurance. Visit homes and create inventory lists of all items, including valuables, furniture collectables etc. Or you could compose a basis inventory list and sell this, so people can add their own belongings as required to the list.

847. What about Writing and selling companies Histories.

848. Offer/start a Staging service for businesses.
Preparing businesses for sale. You could offer a cleaning service, painting and decorating service, de cluttering service etc. Offer a service that will make peoples businesses and premises look presentable for sale. Advertise in your local press/media that you organize home ready for sale.

849. Sell classic car prints by mail order.
Why not buy the prints from poster/print wholesalers, or frame old car prints from magazines. Or why not try your hand at drawing cars, and then selling your drawings on.
TOP TIP: Again, make sure you have resale rights.

850. Provide transportation/chauffeur service for disabled/elderly persons.
You will need a specially adapted vehicle that accommodates wheelchair access. Offer to organise day trips etc, and check what rules, regulations, licenses apply in your area.

851. Hire out skips.
Target both individuals and small businesses, find a regular supply of customers and arrange a contract with a skip hire firm to supply an agreed amount of skips per month to addresses you specify. You basically make money being a middle man or woman.
PROS: This service and product is always in demand.
CONS: You may face some stiff competition.

852. Hire our keep fit/gym equipment.
This could include items such as exercise bikes, rowing machines and home gyms can be hired out for a specified period, to cater for people who would prefer to work out at home rather than go to a gym.
TOP TIP: You could sell health supplements and perhaps workout DVDs at the same time as arranging delivery of the fitness equipment.

853. How about cleaning drives?
Peoples drives get muddy, dirty, icy and so on, why not offer to clean drives for people and local businesses.
TOP TIP: You could offer this service alongside other cleaning services from wheelie bin cleaning to gutter/drain cleaning.

854. Why not offer a College homework editing, research service.

855. Open a pet hotel.
This is a bit like a boarding kennel, but for owners who are going away for maybe a weekend and want there dogs to live/stay in luxury. You could start small, perhaps by converting a spare room in your house into a 5 star doggy hotel room.

856. Be a retirement specialist.
How about helping people plan their retirements, help them decide what they are going to do, how much money they will have etc.

TOP TIP: Why not offer to produce a specialist retirement plan (for a fee of course) which may cover: there disposable income, there incoming and outgoings.

857. Live a second life.
You can create and sell products, start your own business and Even earn money, all from the comfort of your home, so why not take a look at www.secondlife.com

858. Offer a canning service for businesses.
How about targeting small businesses e.g. home run businesses who produce products such as jams, sauces, creams and gels. You could buy you cans and jars from wholesalers and manufacturers and either do the canning yourself, or perhaps you could sell the product required for canning onto the businesses and make a small profit in the process.

TOP TIP: Check out what health and hygiene requirements may apply to you, as well as what licenses you may require in order to can products.

859. How about being a Herbalist.

860. Start a business dedicated to and focusing on Students.
This could for example be to do with selling second hand text books, organising student parties, student events, competitions etc, the list is endless.

TOP TIP: Advertise at colleges and universities, as well as online on student websites.

861. Sell mailing lists, become a mail list broker.
Lots of companies rent mailing lists for use in their direct mail advertising campaigns. Many firms who sell mailing lists either sell them by direct mail themselves or through mail order advertising.
TOP TIP: The easiest way to get started is to compile your own.

862. Become a stockbroker
Why not train to be a stockbroker, join a stock broking firm as an apprentice, learn the ropes, move up then move out, work on your own and take commissions for creating and making deals.

863. Start a company that organises internships for university/school/college leavers.

864. Start a mobile snack bar.
All types of food trailers are available, suitable for selling all kinds of foods/snacks. Sell chips, sandwiches and so on.
TOP TIP: Check with your local council what regulations as to what licences, rules and regulations are in place.

865. Start a telephone answering service for local Businesses.
Some businesses may be home based, and so may require another telephone line (which could be you) or other businesses may require a telephone line for out of office callers. Advertise at your local business centres, and include how much you charge alongside what services you offer.

866. Start a business that sells gadgets that help people in everyday life.
An example of these gadgets could be stress busting gadgets, timesaving gadgets and so on. You could advertise in local magazines, sell online or through mail order.

867. Start a motorbike rental company.
This is ideal if you are in a built up area or a city, both tourists and even locals may find this service appealing. Or as above you could become an affiliate for a large bike rental company.
TOP TIP: Find out what insurance is required, what responsibilities you hold, and what training may be required on your part, if any.

868. Open a gym specifically for women.
You could offer workouts that target women's problem areas for example Tums and bums workout sessions could be offered in lunch hours. If you didn't fancy opening a gym you could always offer just classes specifically for women, say at your local community centre/village hall etc.

869. Start a travelling play bus for children.
How about converting an old Double Decker bus into a playhouse that could perhaps stop at different places different times of the week, at playgroups, village halls, schools, housing estates etc.
PROS: It's creative and bound to catch people's attention
CONS: Insurance, costs to start the play bus.

870. Hold self defence classes for women and children.
You could hold this weekly, or how about once or twice a week. Advertise in your local newspapers, at schools, workplaces on notice boards and at supermarkets.
TOP TIP: Check out what regulations you have to apply and follow for holding these classes.

871. Organise treasure hunts in your local area.
What about organising one off events, you could co operate with other local businesses/companies so that you can share the costs, you can then earn money from entrance fees and participation fees.

872. Produce a weekly or fortnightly newspaper/leaflet for children and parents.
This could provide parents with a guide to what's going on in your local area. When and how much it will cost. You could earn money from advertisers.
TOP TIP: Break the guide down into age specific sections.

873. Become a comedian / hold stand up shows.
Do you think your funny? if so have you though about writing your own material, perhaps based on everyday life, and organise your own gigs. Remember that everybody is funny in their own way.
PROS: Creative way for you to make some money.
CONS: Time consuming initially coming up with material.

874. How about selling lingerie and underwear for larger men and women.
You could sell these items/products through mail order, online, online auctions via home parties etc. You could offer home parties/party plan, and get people to sell for you. You could even design and sell your own lingerie/underwear, and sell it through wholesale to local shops, boutiques.

875. Help people get out of debt.
Why not help people get out of debt, offer a counselling service, charge them for helping them fill out forms, debt consolidation, money management and so on, people will much rather pay you for a useful service than stay in debt.
PROS: Someone is always in debt, and most likely they could do with a helping hand to sort out their finances.
CONS: You may have to dedicate a substantial amount of Time to each client, dependant on the debt/size and type.

876. Write and sell songs.

Have you got a song or two in you. If so then why not write a song, you could place adverts in music magazines, sell your songs online, why not try eBay and other auction websites, build up a reputation for yourself and you can build up your income at the same time.

TOP TIP: Why not teach people how to write songs, or how and where to look for inspiration.

877. Sell hair pieces/wigs.

You could do this through either online, mail order, or both. People often don't like going to buy pieces in a physical shop due to the embarrassment factor, so why not sell these products to them in the comfort of their own homes.

878. Pose as a life/nude model.

If you are happy with your body and figure then go for it, pose and get paid. To find work and jobs start by looking and talking to your local art colleges, look through your local press, and look online to find opportunities.

TOP TIP: Always ring and find out about the job/modelling before agreeing anything, as not all work will be paid and genuine.....be careful.

879. Buy and sell second hand computers.

880. Learn how to face paint.

These don't have to be masterpieces as long as you can get hold of some face paint, you can give it a go. Advertise and get in touch with local entertainers/children's entertainers/place adverts in free newspapers/classifieds.

881. Organise adventure weekends for children.

These are things that help them team build, meet new people and try new things, what adventure parks are there you can organise/base trips around. When organising trips, include all food supplements etc to generate even more income.

PROS: Gives you satisfaction of seeing children lead healthier more active lifestyles, at the same time as earning you some money.

CONS: You will have to check regulations specific to your activities, for example what is the ratio of staff to children, what insurance is required etc.

882. Sell furniture from abroad.

Why not start and import/export service or why not offer a service whereby you source furniture from overseas for private buyers.

TOP TIP: Why not organise overseas furniture shopping trips for people, you could charge people for your knowledge and experience.

883. Sell organic produce/food.

You could have a go at making your own organic food, or set up a restaurant/takeaway/mail order/online shop (whichever you fancy) to sell organic food.

TOP TIP: Search organic recipes on the internet, and if you get into it, why not create an organic cookbook.

884. Help people find volunteering/work placements abroad.

Help find contacts abroad for students for example working in orphanages, charge the student a placement fee, which will cover your costs of arranging the placement, and should leave you with a bit of profit.

885. Start a monogramming service.

886. Hold a car wash or offer to regularly wash people's cars.
Could you do this from your home, if not find a suitable location that you can rent weekly, for example a car park and you should soon build up regular customers.
PROS: You could build up a regular income.
CONS: You may get a bit dirty.

887. Sell old public house/brewery merchandise.
Source products from scrap yards, auction houses, online sites, charity shops etc, and then advertise and sell on to private customers. Since public houses are becoming a thing of the past these items will surely soon be in demand.

888. Set up a professional renting/sharing agency.
You could for example target working professionals who want to share a house or apartment. You can earn money from people placing adverts and subscribing to the site, as well as advertisers paying to advertise on your website/in your agency.
PROS: You're helping people find accommodation and providing local knowledge.
CONS: It may take time to build up a good solid reputation alongside trust.

889. Why not organise auctions.

890. Become a waiter or a waitress.
Or perhaps you could join a professional waitressing service, that deals with more corporate events, functions and so on.

891. Become a job scout or a head-hunter.
You could either work freelance or for a handful of exclusive clients. You job is to help clients source employees, and get paid a referral fee. You could ask for a months wage slip or perhaps similar as your payment/referral fee. This of course depends on what type of employee you find.

892. Become a golf caddy.
Why not ring up all of your local golf courses and see what they need, start at the bottom if you need to and work your way up the ladder to get where you want to be.
TOP TIP: Research how much caddies are paid, and set a price/rate for what you think you deserve and why.

893. Why not sell organic clothing from babies to adults.

894. Open a second hand shop.
Sell anything from clothes to children's toys. You could start this from home, or even offer an online service.
PROS: Low start-up costs.
CONS: Finding products that are suitable for resale may be time consuming.

895. Be a jewellery designer.
Why not have a go at making and selling your jewellery or why not just sell your designs to jewellers. If you decide that you want to make your own jewellery have a look at courses at your local college. You could sell your work at arts and crafts fairs, online or through mail order.

896. Offer a gutter cleaning service.
This is a job that everyone needs done at one time or another but no one is ever around to do it, why not be the person who is around. Advertise your service along with your rates in local free newspapers, and your business should build up. Clean up leaves and get paid for doing it.
TOP TIP: Always carry around a spare pair of gloves.

897. Sell past exam papers to students.
How about getting hold of exam papers, contact examination boards, and then sell exam papers to school students, college and university students. Advertise in the local press, at schools and colleges etc.
PROS: Students always want and sometimes benefit from past examination papers.
CONS: Sourcing previous examination papers.

898. Offer stress management, and stress buster Classes.
Go on be a stress buster, learn how to cope with stress in everyday life and work, and then pass on your knowledge, and make some money in the process.
TOP TIP: Works best if you are not as stressed or highly strung person.

899. Open an ink cartridge filling business.
In addition to this why not offer a cartridge disposal service whereby you go round local businesses and houses and dispose of their empty cartridges. You can find buyers for your empty cartridges or recycle them. Or if you wanted you could start a franchise, such as Cartridge world for example.

900. Be a concert promoter.
Get in touch with music companies to see what concerts/gigs are coming up in your local area, and offer to promote them (for a fee of course) or you could do the same with bands.
PROS: You get to promote and perhaps visit concerts and gigs.
CONS: You may not always get to choose or like who and what you have to promote.

Chapter 18 - How to advertise ideas, businesses or services.

No matter what you do, you always need to let people know you exist. There are a number of ways you can promote your money making ideas, businesses and services, here are 9 to get you started

1. Advertise through Word of mouth.
This is free, and invaluable, word of mouth is the best marketing method to use. Get people talking about your product, idea, service or business, tell family, friends, acquaintances, and work colleagues. Spread the word.

2. Send out Press Releases.
Send out Press Releases to your local press and media. Make the press release factual, more news than sales copy. Tell the press why they should be interested in you and what you are doing.

3.Use you email dares.
Put your business/information in your email signature line, its free promotion !

4. Use leaflets and flyers.
Again these are very cheap, as you can produce them on your computer and distribute to your target areas yourself.
Remember to not cram the leaflet with writing and information, leave white space to make your leaflet more appealing and effective.

5. Use Business cards.
Get some business cards produced, hand them out to people you meet, at networking events, give a few to family and friends to do the same.

6. Get a website or blog.
Tell the whole world what you are up to, hat you are planning, advertising, selling and so on. Remember to include your website address, or blog address on every piece of promotional/marketing material you send out,

7. Start your own newsletter.
Why not start a newsletter focusing on or around your idea/service or business.

8. Use Free classifieds and Free for all links pages.
To find free classified sites to advertise one simply type free classifieds into your favourite search engine.

9. Write articles
Go on, write some articles on subjects you know about, submit them to websites needing content. Always remember to put a link to your web page at the bottom of your article and some contact information, or just some information about you and what you do.

Chapter 19 - Ways to make money 901 -1001

901. Start an e-zine on the internet.
This is an online magazine/newsletter. You can earn money by charging a subscription, or by placing advertisers adverts, An e-zine is delivered via a Web site or an email newsletter.

902. Start a carpet cleaning business.
You will need cleaning equipment that is suitable for upholstery cleaning as well as carpets is necessary.
PROS: There are always carpets that need cleaning.
CONS: Working out how much time you will need for each job.

903. How about Starting a caravan/camp site.

904. Start a garden maintenance service.
Build up a regular round of customers whose gardens need to be kept in good order. Include services such as weed control, pruning, and lawn mowing. Advertise door to door with leaflets, flyers and through word of mouth. Offer your services to both individuals and businesses.

905. Buy and sell used computers.
Place adverts in your local newspapers to both buy and sell used computers, sell used and refurbished computers on online auctions, and through word of mouth/flyer advertising.
TOP TIP: Search for businesses that are closing down and selling off stock.

906. Be a driving instructor.
In the UK if you are over 21 and have at least three years driving experience on a full licence you could train to become a driving instructor.

PROS: Flexible hours, and good money.

CONS: You will need to be calm, patient and understanding.

907. Design and print certificates.
For example you could try your hand at printing sports certificates, school certificates and so on. Promote through mail order, or direct mail, contact schools and businesses to let them know you exist and what you charge etc.

908. Start your own mobile advertising company.
A large van or something of similar size/proportions can be used to advertise firms in your local area. Charge a daily weekly or monthly fee for as long as you advertise the company/business. Charge fees dependant on how long the client wants to advertise, and the size of their advertisements.

TOP TIP: Advertise your services at local business centres, as well as getting leaflets/flyers and business cards printed up, and handed out.

909. Become a sales representative.
For one or several companies, such as a party planning company, or maybe even a mail order company, whereby you put on a party for clients and then sell the products shown at the party.

910. Start Offering typing services, do this from your own home to reduce costs and overheads.

911. Buy and sell personalised/cherished number plates

Private number plates are really popular, you could buy number plates at auction and resell while advertising for more plates to buy. Check the transfer regulations and become familiar with the documentation required. Some plates can be worth a small fortune.

TOP TIP: Build up your selection for sale and advertise in motor magazines, Exchange & Mart and Auto trader.

912. Organise second hand books sales.

No book buying and selling required, all you do is organise. Hire a small hall, set up some stalls and invite people to sell their old book collections. Charge a small entrance fee and a basic charge to stallholders. Where possible, organise a place for visitors to sit down and provide suitable refreshments.

PROS: Always popular with people of all ages.

CONS: Getting the word around to sellers (perhaps based in other areas) may be quite time consuming.

913. Why not start a Custom poem service.

914. Write jokes and letters.

Get paid for sending them into newspapers/magazines – or compose and sell joke books, produce a wide range of jokes that can be used at all occasions.

915. Produce a series of audio cassettes for helping people relax (similar to popular books).

There are books written about stress relief, hypnosis etc, so why not turn this knowledge into spoken knowledge/advice. Buy a product that has resell right and sell sell sell, or if you prefer you could take snippets from old books (where copyright has expired) and devise a script that can be recorded on tape to help people overcome their tension and fears. You could use a professional speaker. Sell the CDs by mail order and in various magazines with a classified ads section

916. Sell science-fiction and fantasy books.
You could sell these products/items almost anywhere. Why
not contact wholesalers and see what they have to offer. You
could sell English and foreign copies of the books at local
markets/fairs, book conventions etc by mail order and also
over the internet.
TOP TIP: Why not place adverts for books wanted, who knows
you might get some for free.

**917. Compose and sell a list of houses and apartments
for rent, locally, regionally or nationally.**

918. How about opening a collector's museum.
This is a unique money making idea and not for the faint
hearted, but it could just work, you could for example
dedicate your museum to a collection of old items that are
remembered and popular with visitors. These could include
artefacts such as Toy trains, dolls houses, film memorabilia or
vintage clothes for example. Earn money by Charging and
entrance fee. Note also that if you didn't want to open a
museum you could organise your very own collectors days
(and then earn money from sellers fees and entrance fees).
You don't have to open a massive museum, for example you
could see if your local shop (related to your museum) has any
spare space that you can rent out.

919. How about starting a business selling self improvement DVDs and CDs.
Sell and aim your products towards individuals. Products could widely vary and could include topics and areas such as titles relating to keeping fit, losing weight/weight loss, self defence, improving your memory etc. With this money making idea you could also target businesses/employees. To drum up ore business you could try repackaging your products as relaxing/productivity products, which for example could help increase staff productivity and efficiency.
PROS: This could be popular, start if from home.
CONS: Knowing which product will suit your market/area (DO SOME MARKET RESEARCH to overcome this con).

920. Start a doggy massage service.

921. Set up and run a mobile discotheque.
Cater for events organisers, private functions, such as engagement parties, wedding reception parties, anniversary parties, birthday parties etc. If you are not much of a DJ then hire one try out a few, see who fits your needs and requirements. Get both flyers and business cards produced and then start handing them out, posting them at local clubs/venues/community centres etc. Get involved in your local music scene, be seen to build up your name and reputation.
PROS: If music is your passion then this is perfect for you, you could target anyone anywhere from university students to wedding parties.
CONS: Unsociable hours and non stop promoting.

922. How about buying and selling toy train sets, including accessories for both enthusiasts and collectors alike.

Trains are mainly for parents and collectors and so advertising in specialist magazines and in your local press may be a good starting point.

Sell your train sets/trains at specialist/collectors fairs.

TOP TIP: Learn to repair/fix broken trains, stations, sets etc.

923. Sell music cassettes, CDs, DVDs and videos from a market stall.

You could sell both new and used products, alongside music merchandise/memorabilia, make sure all your stuff is legitimate and non of it is counterfeit. Buy your stock/items from house clearances, wanted adverts, for sale adverts/wholesalers etc. Move on to selling by mail order and online once you have built up a solid reputation.

924. Start a service buying and selling everything and anything through online auctions.

Sell anything from second hand items to car parts. Whatever you chose to sell research your marketplace, and see what your potential mark-ups can be, then go ahead and do a few test auctions, before listing 100s of items.

PROS: Low cost to setup accounts and get selling, you can source items from anywhere, from car boots to house clearances and wholesalers.

CONS: Items may not sell first time around, and may cost you more to keep listing (Work out each and every profit margin, on any of you products).

925. Start a private taxi hire only for women.

More and more women feel unsafe as to who might be taking them home. Why not offer reassurance, offer a service that's catered to just women.

926. Start a delivery service for people who are housebound/handicapped.
Why not start a small mail order/shopping list. Get together a list of items people may need from time to time, or that people may need on a weekly basis.

927. Train to be a tattoo artist/body piercer.

928. Start a bulletin board advertising service.
Place bulletin boards around your local area and charge people to place ads for example 50p-£1.00 for a week, month etc, based on demand.
TOP TIP: More boards equals more money.

929. Start a clip art business/service.
Collect clip art from all over the world, make sure you have resale rights, and then rent out the clipart, you could for example rent out your art to start-up businesses who require a logo or stationery head.

930. Why not create a hobby newsletter for enthusiasts.
Originate a newsletter or directory for and about hobbyists and their crafts. Build readership by exchanging ideas, listing fairs and supply sources with others online and offline.

931. Start/Offer a Narrating service.
Use your speaking ability to narrate private or commercial movies, videos, demos and advertisements. Sell taped versions for slide show presentations

932. Start a Mattress cleaning service.
Dirty mattresses can cause problems, such as allergies and skin disorders. Buy a second hand mattress cleaner, print up some business cards, leaflets and flyers and away you go, most likely will be a popular business/service.

933. Why not start a Pet café or restaurant.
Create a service/ business whereby pets and their owners can eat together, crazy as it might initially sound. Provide pet menus alongside owner menus, create a separate room/restaurant where all the pets eat. You could even offer a takeaway service, for travelling pets and their owners.

934. Start an agency from home.
This for example could be one that organises that job sharing for placements, and that has job share workers on its books.

935. Turn loneliness into a business.
Start your own social centre/meeting place, charge an entrance fee, and then arrange games, dancing refreshments etc, that will help get other "lonely" people interacting with one another, help people meet new people, place adverts for your meetings in you local press.

936. Offer a Lawn mower maintenance, repair, and clean service.

937. Start and Offer a Get you up on time service.
Perhaps you could charge a monthly or annual fee, to ring peoples homes to wake them up for work, school etc. Advertise your service with flyers, business cards and word of mouth.

938. Be a book reviewer.
Become a book reviewer, read books, review them and then sell you reviews to bookshops, books clubs, and perhaps even publishers.

939. Start a Seminar/Conference service/business.
Conduct business or learning seminars in your area of
expertise or hire experts to cover virtually any subject. Lease
the hall, promote, sell tickets and Snacks.
TOP TIP: Promote other peoples conference and seminars
and earn a cut/commission for every sale you generate.

940. Have you got a website.
If so then why not think of using or adding Amazon affiliate,
Bidvertiser, selling advertising space, joining affiliate
Programs.

941. Mark exam papers.

**942. Start a group/service that helps people pay off
their mortgages early.**
By explaining alternative payment structures to clients (which
can result in a smaller total payment in a shorter period of
Time).

**943. Teach people how to work from home/run a
business from home etc.**

944. Start a Breakfast in Bed service.
Advertise your service through word of mouth. You can offer a
standard breakfast menu, or a custom one for extra, deliver
the breakfasts on certain days and at certain times.

945. Offer Outdoor recreation work.
Include kayaking/white-water rafting outfitter; guided
mountain biking, trekking, backpacking, or rock climbing, be a
tour operator, walking guide and so on.

**946. Why not start up a Washing up service. Target
businesses and individuals.**

947. Invest abroad. Perhaps in stocks and shared, the property market, or local businesses.

948. Why not start a Merchandise/display shop.
Open a show room, for various shops/businesses in your area, for example display products for sale alongside a not where they can be found, charge people to display their items in your store/shop, this can be done with a physical location, or even with an online shop.

949. Why not Start a catering company.

950. Become an Internet DJ.
For example use sites such as Live365.com you can create a new, live or pre-recorded broadcast or relay an existing broadcast to an Internet audience, earn revenue and control your own advertising. By linking to your station from your own website you can give your visitors a treat - and your income too!

951. Why not start/offer a specialised budgeting service.
Help people create budgets for their everyday lives, from individuals to families, or, why not create and sell your own budget sheet, for example how much a family of 5 can live on. *TOP TIP*: This service would be popular around Christmas time.

952. Start a clothing exchange service/business

953. Offer a Transcription service from your home.
Type notes from recorded materials, such as DVDs, tapes, CDs etc. Offer this service to schools/academic institutions, professional writers, small businesses, and legal services.

954. Be a Human billboard.
You could for example for restaurants, cafes etc, businesses
see this as a quirky way to advertise, and you can see it as
cash in hand.

955. Buy and sell old record collections.
Trade in various collections of music including rock, pop, jazz,
classical, rhythm and blues etc. There's still demand for old
LPs and singles, particularly original recordings. Advertise in
local press and in music magazines. Also sell at car boot sales
and collectors fairs.

956. Start a rent a date service.

957. Be a food photographer.
Clients could include catering companies, food magazines,
restaurants, cake decorators, and food manufacturers who
supply the trade.

958. Buy and sell second-hand photographic equipment.
Either set up a shop or sell via the internet. Used equipment
can be advertised as wanted through classified advertising or
bought from auction. Check the online auctions.

**959. Be a public speaker. E.g. you could work for local
businesses.**

960. Create and sell your own bookmarks.
You could sell your bookmarks through souvenir shops,
through mail order, or perhaps through local businesses. Offer
a customisation service, whereby people can create their own
bookmarks.

**961. Buy and rent out holiday caravans. Or help people
rent out their holiday homes.**

962. Start a mobile laundry service.
This would involve building up a regular round of customers who would require their laundry to be collected, cleaned and delivered, preferably the same day. A useful service for busy people, who don't have the time to do this chore themselves, and also the elderly or disabled who need a helping hand.

963. Start a service that organise local business and networking meetings.

964. Why not cook for students.
Offer home cooked meals for underfed students, charging a set amount per meal.

965. Write a book on how you made or how you are making money.

966. Start a business teaching other people how to set up and run a party plan business.
If you have any experience in this field of selling, this could be a good opportunity to help others, who have little or no experience in this area, succeed in their new venture. Offer a one day course for people to develop their skills in the various stages of party planning, from arranging the party, through to presentation, entertaining guests, getting the orders and obtaining more bookings.

967. Start a business that organises a regular nearly new clothing sales event.
Similar to a car boot sale, this would involve hiring a hall, renting stalls to people with clothes to sell, charging a small admission fee and running a small Food and drink facility. Advertise each event in the local press.

968. Be a franchise advisor.
How about advising people on what their options are when it comes to starting or running a franchise, why not help them choose what franchise is best suited to them.

969. Get paid to review businesses and places.
Use dooyoo and get paid 50 pence per valid review you write, you can also get paid 1.5 pence every time some reads and rates your review, so why not visit dooyoo and sign up now to start earning some cash at: www.dooyoo.co.uk

970. How about being a recycling Consultant.

971. Start an ad writing service for both individuals and businesses.
Find work from online businesses, and for example businesses on auction sites, as well as businesses that may regularly place for sale or job adverts.
TOP TIP: Work freelance, and sell your service to everyone you meet, as people may want anything from a housing advert written to a job wanted advert.

972. Start a sign writing business.
Write, create and sell handmade business signs, or design signs for small start up businesses. Lots of possibilities here.

973. Start your own agony aunt or uncle column.

974. Make up and sell hanging baskets.
Sell them by calling on residents who live in upmarket residential areas, through mail order, direct mail, or by holding hanging basket sales in your back garden.
TOP TIP: To get yourself noticed why not carry your hanging Baskets around in a brightly painted handcart or a suitable small van.

975. Be an external painter.
If you've ever painted a room, then you can paint an exterior. Target both small local businesses and private individuals. Advertise through leaflets, word of mouth, and in your local classifieds.

976. Start a mailing service for direct mail advertisers.
This would involve combining a selection of leaflets or cards advertising various products and services that might appeal to the general public, or names from a specified mailing list. After placing the advertising material together in one professionally designed envelope, the mailing is sent to prospective customers. The fee for this service would be approximately half the cost incurred to advertisers preparing and sending out their own mail shot.

977. Write books on successful people and how they achieved their wealth and success.

978. Why not Start a mobile karaoke business.
Like mobile discos, the karaoke machine has found popularity as a means of spicing up private parties and regular weekly pub night entertainment. Advertise your services through the local press and Yellow Pages.

979. Breed and sell tropical fish.
Equipment can be a little expensive to begin with. Some types of tropical fish can bring good profits and are worth persevering with. You can sell them through various pet stores or directly to the public through classified Advertisements.

980. Why not start making and selling home made ice cream.

981. How about starting a night time day care/nursery/babysitting service.
Offer a night time Day care service. Take care of two or three children in this way a few nights a week will prove very lucrative.

982. Why not Start a plant rental business.
Rent plants out for such events as weddings

983.Start a screen-printing service.
How about printing t-shirts, jumpers etc, for local schools, businesses and organisations.

984. Supply, fit, replace, repair both television aerials and satellite dishes.
You could supply, repair and fit aerials, fix brackets to walls, and chimneys, and away you go. Advertise in your local classified/local telephone directory, the Yellow Pages and your local newspaper as well as in pubs, community centres.

985. Hold Aerobic classes.
Why not hold them in your house, in your garage, or perhaps at a local community centre, village hall, and charge say £5.00 per person per class they attend. Advertise in your local press/media and local shops and supermarkets.
PROS: You can keep fit, and hold different types of aerobic classes, for example from catering to pregnant women to aerobics for children, or even the elderly.
CONS: Local regulations may decide which line of aerobics you want to pursue.

986.Print and sell commercial and industrial signs.
For example signs such as No Entry or No Smoking, sell these to local businesses as well as to start-up companies.
Advertise in business centres as well as in your local business press.

987.Sell prints and reproductions of famous sites and buildings. From sketches to watercolours.

988. Why not start a swap shop, make money from charging an entrance fee.

989. Why not start your own baby/kids club/Tot Library.
Charge a monthly or an annual fee to parents, and offer a service whereby parent and children attend a mini book club, and exchange books, toys, games etc. Provide play afternoons, as well as renting out the games and books to parents for one week for example.

990. Print and sell animal prints and photographs.
Sell yourself as well as through local shops/businesses, sell sketches, paintings and photographs.

991. Be search engine optimization specialist.
If you are a bit of a whiz on the computer why not be/offer a freelance Search engine marketing/optimization service, particularly aimed and target towards small start-up companies.

992. TV/Electrical/Appliances repair.
Repair electrical appliances from microwaves to TVs, or possibly contract the work out and make money in the process.

993. Why not start a baby goods swap shop or similar.
A Pushchair Exchange might also be possible. Many mothers in the lower income brackets would be keen to buy second hand baby goods, products and items.

994. Try your hand at making and selling kites.
You can sell these through mail order, through a website, through affiliate links on other websites, through advertising on other peoples websites, through school, fetes, fairs and even made to order through word of mouth.

995. Start a celebrity/look-alike agency.
Why not produce and place adverts for look-alikes, get look a likes on your books and then get promoting to business/event organisers, charge a commission to both the look alike, and the event organiser.
PROS: Impersonators and look-alikes are always in demand, and there is potentially a good profit/mark up to be made.
CONS: Finding suitable look-alikes may take more time than you first anticipated.

996. Why not be a Chiropractor.

997. Become a famous/celebrity look-alike.
Do you look like anyone famous? Could you be a celebrity look-alike? Could you attend events pretending to be a famous person/celebrity? Why not join an agency, or go it alone and find work for yourself.

998. Start a bed and breakfast.
This is and ideal opportunity if you live in a tourist area. You have to be friendly, and your home need to be clean and habitable. Guests require access to a bathroom, as well as a well laid out breakfast. Advertise through word of mouth, in bed and breakfast guides, on forums, on websites, and in your front window.
TOP TIP: Offer activities in addition to your bed and breakfast, for example walking holidays, horse riding, shopping trips to bring in additional income.

999. Become an apartment/flat locator.
You could work for both the estate agencies and for individuals in search of a new home, find apartments for rent and for sale, make contacts in local communities/areas and charge a commission to either individuals or companies who take up your offer.

1000. Draw and sell cartoons.
Are you artistic, could you for example draw and sell your artwork/cartoons/funnies to local publications and local newspapers. Invent a cartoon character or set of them which appeals to people of all ages. Produce regular short comic strips to get people interested.

1001. Why not be a Crystal therapist.

Chapter 20 - Some extra ways to make money.

As if that wasn't enough here are a few more ways to make money.

1002. Buy and sell painted and/or stained glass.
You could also paint and sell you own if you wanted. If you want to buy older stained pieces you can source these from scrap yards, house clearances, local markets and car boots.
TOP TIPS: Offer a customisation service, whereby people can choose what they want in their window/door. If you feel you cannot do this why not design stained glass doors/windows for people then take the design to a glazier to get it produced, then sell it on.

1003. Why not train to be a Healer.

1004. Make/paint and sell garden gnomes and other garden ornaments.
You could sell direct to customers, approach local garden centres to stock your products, sell on a market stall, through mail order or even on online. You could even offer paint your own gnome classes to generate even more income.
PROS: Relatively low cost to produce, paint etc.
CONS: Not everyone's cup of tea.

1005. Produce and sell novelty film posters and gifts.

1006. Make and sell dolls houses.
If you didn't fancy this you could always make and sell your own dolls house kits, or buy these kits and sell on. You could also offer a service whereby you construct dolls houses. If you didn't want to stop there you could also sell the dolls, and dolls house furniture.
TOP TIP: This money making idea could have a large target market as it caters to both the young and old.

1007. Why not start offering baby massage classes.

1008. Why not have a go at Forex Trading

1009. How about dressing houses to sell.
Some houses just don't look appealing to buyers, as
some buyers just cant see past old wallpaper and so
on. So why not offer to go in to houses that have
been on the market for while, clean them, use the
furniture that is in the house, move it around and
just freshen the whole house up ready for sale.
TOP TIP: Advertise this service in local estate agents and
in your local press and media.

**1010. Why not have a go at buying and selling costume
jewellery.**

1011. Why not be a Tarot card reader/fortune teller.
If you are good at palmistry or tarot reading, give
performances at parties, fairs and at a mall booth and at
festivals. Sell booklets, card kits, offer your tarot services for
entertainment purposes only.

1012. Make and sell bird boxes.

1013. Create eBook Year books.

Chapter 21 - How to develop your money making ideas

Everybody has ideas, it is how they are created and developed that makes them into profitable/money making ideas.

There are 3 main ways you can create and develop money making ideas.

The first is by looking at the existing products market, what are they missing, what will make it better, faster, more reliable etc.

The second is to improve or alter current products in the marketplace.

The third is to invent a completely new product/service

TOP TIPS FOR DEVELOPING IDEAS:

• Write down all of your ideas, no matter how silly they may sound, as later on you could turn these ideas into money.

• If ideas don't naturally come to you throughout your day for example, why not look at products and think about how each one could be better, think about what you do each and everyday and what could improve how you do each and everyday, what could save you money, time, effort etc.

• Whether you are putting into practice one of the ideas from this book, or putting your own idea into practice, analyse the idea, and ask yourselves such as: How much will it cost to get the idea into action, how long until its profitable, is it is a new idea, or is it an improvement on existing idea. Does your idea solve a problem?

Chapter 22 - Useful Contacts / Websites

Here are some useful websites that you might benefit from visiting, using and signing up to. Start making money RIGHT NOW with the links below.

A top site to visit for free information, articles and much more.
www.1001waystomakemoney.co.uk

A very useful, resourceful and necessary place to go for all your home working needs.
www.homeworking.com

Another great site to make money from while your on the internet - JOIN FOR FREE
http://www.ecasher.co.uk/?rpid=596

A great business opportunity
www.my-mag-uk.com

1001 free money making and money saving articles
www.associatedcontent.com/user/62651/l_j_pearce.html

Get paid to write reviews`, review places and products
www.dooyoo.co.uk

Earn money while you are online, join this site now
JOIN FOR FREE
http://www.e-cashrewards.com?referer=lauzpauz

Blog of the Author L J Pearce, 1001 ways to make money
http://ljpearce.blogspot.com

Get paid to go shopping
www.retaileyes.co.uk

A search engine that pays you for searching - sign up now
JOIN FOR FREE
http://www.myhpf.co.uk/apply001.asp?Friend=2940

The best place to start for all your blogging needs
www.blogger.com

A very useful, helpful and essential site for all the stoozers
www.stoozing.com

A very good site for all the freelancers out there
www.freelanceuk.com

Another top site to join to make more on the internet
JOIN FOR FREE
http://www.cashinco.co.uk/index.php?refID=1600170

Brilliant site where you can earn money for writing
JOIN FOR FREE
http://www.squidoo.com/lensmaster/referral/ljpearce

A Top site if you want to make some extra money while your
online -JOIN FOR FREE
http://www.TopCashBack.co.uk/lauzpauz/ref/index.html

BOOK ORDER FORM

You can order further copies of this book direct from Hillside Publishing.

DELIVERY ONLY £2.50 NO MATTER HOW MANY BOOKS ORDERED

To order further copies of 1001 ways to make money please send a copy of the coupon below to:

Hillside Publishing
66 Hillside Road
Linton
Swadlincote
DE12 6QW

Alternatively, you may download an order form from our website: www.1001waystomakemoney.co.uk

✂ --

Please send me ____ copies of 1001 ways to make money.

☐   I enclose a UK bank cheque or postal order, payable to Hillside Publishing for £_____ @ £14.99 per copy.

NAME:

ADDRESS:

POSTCODE:

☐   Please allow 28 days for delivery. Do not send cash. Offer subject to availability. We do not share or sell our customers details. Please tick box if you do not wish to receive further information from Hillside Publishing.